KT-464-867

JACK EDWARDS

THE
UNI-VERSE

THE ULTIMATE UNIVERSITY
SURVIVAL GUIDE

HarperCollins*Publishers*

This book is dedicated to my A Level Biology teacher,
who told me it was 'time to start aiming lower'
— I'm glad I didn't.

HarperCollins*Publishers*
1 London Bridge Street
London SE1 9GF

www.harpercollins.co.uk

First published by HarperCollins*Publishers* 2020

3 5 7 9 10 8 6 4

Text © Jack Edwards 2020
Illustrations: page 114 © Shutterstock.com; page 132 © Liane Payne

Jack Edwards asserts the moral right to be
identified as the author of this work

A catalogue record of this book is
available from the British Library

ISBN 978-0-00-836564-6

Printed and bound in Great Britain by
CPI Group (UK) Ltd, Croydon

MIX
Paper from
responsible sources
FSC™ C007454

This book is produced from independently certified FSC™ paper
to ensure responsible forest management.

For more information, visit: www.harpercollins.co.uk/green

CONTENTS

INTRODUCTION

Hey! My name is Jack Edwards and I've just finished my final year studying English Literature at Durham University. This is *The Uni-Verse* – my ultimate guide to university, sharing an *actual* student's perspective. From dressing as a jellyfish using only bubble wrap and tape to setting my microwave on fire with a single piece of bread, I've really done it all, and with this book I hope to impart all the wisdom I've gained … conflagration not included.

So, whether you're looking for housemates to live with or tips and tricks to help avoid murdering them, this is your complete, unadulterated, unfiltered survival guide with all the trimmings. Just think of me as the Bear Grylls of university. Except I've never been on a rugby club bar crawl, so I've never actually had to drink my own urine.

I was the first in my immediate family to go to university, so I had pretty much no idea what I was doing when I applied. There were so many questions bubbling away in my brain, and a dearth of useful information online. It's safe to say that, when

I first packed my bags and left for university, I was an incompetent monkey (my parents would almost too eagerly agree) … I truly put the 'fun' in *fun*damentally incapable. I'd like to think that I actually know what I'm doing now (my parents may not so eagerly agree on this one) and I've had the most incredible time working it all out. This is the book I would've wanted to read three years ago before I embarked on the academic heptathlon that is university, and that's why I'm so passionate about writing it. Also, I'm an English Lit student, so this is pretty much a dream come true.

This book includes everything I think you need to know, including what to pack, what to expect from your first day/ week/term, how to pay rent, and the all-important question: how the hell do you keep houseplants alive? Seriously, how do you expect to keep yourself alive if you have the carcass of a rotting succulent on your bookshelf? I've got you covered.

CHAPTER 1

BEFORE YOU GO TO UNIVERSITY

So, you want to go to university? Amazing! There are a few things you need to do before you find yourself in the lecture hall (or the nightclub) on day one of Freshers' Week, so I've dedicated the first section of this book to the pre-uni hustle. After all, there's a personal statement to write, the emotional roller coaster that is UCAS Track and the small matter of exams to get through first. And we all know the 'h' in exam season stands for 'happiness' ...

How to pick your course

Of course, the first thing you should think about when applying to go to university is *drum roll please* the course you'll be studying! It's so crucial that you get this right and opt for something that you're genuinely passionate about, because you've got to live, breathe and sleep it (or, indeed, get-no-sleep-and-pull-an-all-nighter it) for three, four or even more years.

And the key word there is *you*. Your subject has to be something *you* care about. Not what your parents think will lead to a successful career that they can brag about to strangers they meet on dog walks. Not what your teachers tell you you're destined to study because you pretend you know what's going on in class surprisingly convincingly. Not what your horoscope suggests you'd be good (or Sagit-terrible) at. You don't want to be the one left picking up the Pisces.

It's about what you know you enjoy. It's about studying the thing that is going to wake you up in the morning and excite you.

The best way to get an insight into what a course entails is by checking different university department websites. Often they'll have full breakdowns of what each year of the course expects of you and the content they cover.

If there are a few different subjects that you particularly enjoyed or excelled in during your GCSEs, A Levels, BTECs or IB years, and you can't quite pick one, then investigate all of them. There's no harm in not knowing just yet, and no shame in testing the water of a few different subjects at this initial stage. It can be hard narrowing down your options – it's like picking your favourite *Friends* character. Although we all know no one's favourite is Ross.*

Alternatively, there's always the safety-net option of taking what's known as 'combined honours', which means you study multiple subjects. If you opt for this, it's probably a good idea to take two subjects that complement each other (like History and Politics, Maths and Physics, or English and Psychology), but that's not to say that other combinations aren't valid, too. In fact, the more obscure the combination you go for, the more nuanced and unique your research and dissertation could be – although that's a pretty intense, long-term investment in a 12,000-word essay.

At open days, it's definitely a good idea to go to subject talks, where a professor will give a presentation on the experience you can expect from a specific degree. If there are multiple subjects that you're toying with then go to all the different subject presentations, and that should make it pretty clear to you which one excites you the most. I certainly found it useful for narrowing down my options.

Reading lists and lecture breakdowns** should be available online via faculty websites and will be invaluable in your

---

* Disclaimer: I mean that no one's favourite *Friends* character is the palaeontologist Ross, who has more divorces than cats have lives … not just any normal person called Ross. I'm sure other people called Ross are lovely.

** The idea of 'lecture breakdowns' is something you will become very familiar with over the course of your degree, in a very different context to the one I'm referring to here.

decision-making. Also, every uni is different and creates their own unique modules, as well as a different way of studying (and examining) the subject, so it's worth casting your net pretty wide at first.

Another thing to look out for is a subject that you've never had a chance to study before, especially those that link to the subjects you have taken previously. Not everyone will have had the opportunity to study things like Anthropology, Geology or Film before university, but one of them may actually be the course you're best suited to. Often course documents/guides will suggest some traditional subjects that facilitate these more specific degrees – for example, a background in Biology or History would complement an Anthropology* degree perfectly. *Italian chef kiss*

I suppose the main point here is that picking the right course for you to study should be your number-one priority, because it's the thing that will envelope your life for the foreseeable future. No subject is too niche, or too broad, or too hard, or too easy, regardless of what anyone tells you. Pursue what is going to intrigue and fascinate you, because it's going to be an enormous part of your university experience.

---

* Anthropology is the study of human cultures and societies and their development. I will confess, I had never even heard of this before going to uni and coming face to face with budding anthropologists. To be totally honest, I'm still not 100 per cent sure what it entails. However, it most definitely does exist and sounds fascinating! Just make sure you can spell it.

Open days and picking the perfect university

On open days, universities 'open' their doors to allow prospective students to have a mooch around and suss out their potential new home. I remember being very self-conscious on open days, because I felt like the bigwigs at the uni were watching my every move and waiting for me to give them a reason not to accept me. One thing I thought I'd tell you straight away is that nothing you do on the open day will have an impact on your chances of getting in … unless you kill someone.

Open days are for *you*. They're for the university to show off their facilities and try to entice you into applying. This is their chance to win you over. That's why they practically throw freebies at prospective pupils.

Things you should consider when picking a university

1. **Location:** How far away from home is it?* Is the commute to/from this location easy or complicated?

* I should add that distance is actually much less of a big deal than you may first think. I moved 350 miles away from home for university and was terrified, but actually, once you're there, you totally forget about the distance. I didn't apply to unis that were in Scotland because it felt too far from home, and I regretted it massively. It's also great to experience a brand-new part of the country that isn't anywhere near home.

8

What other cities are nearby?

2. **Grade expectations:** What grades do the universities expect from you? I'd recommend applying to at least one uni that is quite ambitious, and at least two that are safe bets (as in, you know you're likely to get the grades they'd expect of you).

3. **Accommodation:** What are the different types of accommodation available? How close to the campus or university buildings are they? What's the bathroom situation? What's the kitchen/common area like?

4. **Campus/city:** Campus universities are very self-contained, and usually a bus ride away from the city. They'll have accommodation, department buildings and probably a club all in one central hub. City universities have their academic facilities dotted around, so you get to actually live in the city centre.

5. **Catered/self-catered:** Lots of unis have the option to be catered in your first year (meaning your meals are cooked for you and served in a dining hall) – this can be very sociable and ameliorates one of those initial living-alone stresses of having to cook for yourself. Being self-catered, however, gives you lots more independence and flexibility, and is also cheaper. Pick whichever suits you best.

6. **Facilities:** If you're training to play tennis at Wimbledon, it's probably pretty crucial that your uni has a tennis court. Make sure the one you pick has the facilities you need: a gym; access to a swimming pool; study spaces etc.

7. **Opportunities:** The student experience is obviously key. Make sure all your dreams for uni are going to be satisfied, for example by ski trips, volunteering projects and charity challenges like Jailbreak.

8. **Careers:** What links does the university have to your ideal career path? Will they set you up with the right contacts? For example, if you're hoping to study media or film, a specialist university with connections to those industries is going to be more beneficial to you than, say, a Russell Group institution.

9. **Culture:** Edinburgh has the Fringe, Manchester and London are cultural capitals, Brighton and Newcastle have wild nights out. Do some research to see what life in the city is like, and what events they have going on.

Make sure you ask loads of questions. Remember all the students volunteering at open days have given up their time to be there, and want to help you. They also aren't trying to sell the uni to you and so will be as brutally honest as they can be.

Also, take photos! There's a big time gap between open days and results day when you find out if your place is confirmed, and you'll appreciate the reminders of what the accommodation and facilities look like. Plus, all the universities you visit tend to kind of merge into one in your head, so photos are useful reminders of which is which.

Check if you need tickets to visit certain accommodation or university buildings, as some are so popular that the uni has to regulate how many people are inside at each time. All info will be on the university website.

My top tip would be to keep track of your opinions on each university by having a score sheet on your phone. Rate each one on the accommodation, the facilities and all the other aspects I spoke about above, and then you'll have a quantitative way of comparing them. My parents also kept their own score sheets and we'd sit and compare them after each open day, as I appreciated having a second (or third) opinion.

An example score sheet would be:

	Uni 1	Uni 2	Uni 3	Uni 4	Uni 5
Accommodation					
Facilities					
Opportunities					
Location					
Course					

How to write a killer personal statement

So, how do you write the perfect personal statement without, on the one hand, sounding arrogant and self-congratulatory or, on the other, underselling yourself and seeming a bit unimpressive. How do you prove your undying passion for a subject you most likely picked out of a process of elimination? How do you reference texts, and do you need to bother actually reading them? I've been to *countless* talks at top universities about how to concoct the perfect personal statement and so, with this guide, I've got you covered. Also, spoiler alert, YES, FOR THE LOVE OF GOD, YOU SHOULD DEFINITELY HAVE READ THE TEXTS YOU MENTION.

(Note: These are personal statements that are *killer* in the positive sense – they pack a punch; a knockout blow assured to secure your space at the uni of your dreams. They are not personal statements for killers. We're not applying to be the next Ted Bundy. Even if the process of writing a personal statement can be *Extremely Wicked, Shockingly Evil and Vile.*)*

---

* This might be the first (and last) time someone brings up a Zac Efron film in a guide to personal statements, but I'm delighted that my book will have this accolade. Zac and I actually share a birthday – sadly the only thing we have in common …

The essentials

Think of your personal statement as an essay, only it's an essay on yourself. It's a way of showing an admissions officer – who, by the way, just wants you to make their job easier – what you're about and why you're the best thing since someone had the ingenious idea of putting peanuts *inside* M&M's. (Seriously, where's their Nobel Prize?)

1. **Remember what information has already been covered in the rest of your application.** When you apply to a university, it's not *just* your personal statement that is sent to them. There's also the rest of your UCAS application, which includes a reference from your school or sixth form, and a full transcript of your academic record. It'll tell the admissions officer about all the grades you have acquired over the years, and contextualise them with the school you went to and the area you grew up in. For this reason, you don't need to flaunt your past grades (or your target grades for the future) in your personal statement. If you got an A in your Maths GCSE – or 7/8/9 for those studying under the new system – which will suggest your suitability for a Maths degree, then the admissions staff will already know. Don't waste valuable space by inserting each grade you're proud of one-by-one and the circumstances in which you achieved them. You'll only be repeating yourself.

2. **The 'academic versus non-academic' split ...**
    Remember that this is an essay proving your academic ability and aptness for a particular academic programme. I'm repeating the word *academic* here intentionally, because it truly is the most important thing to focus on. With this in mind, your personal statement should be *at least* 70 per cent focused on your scholarly ability, insights and flare. Basically, talk about your subject and why it fascinates you. What areas are you most intrigued by? How have you researched the subject outside of the standard curriculum? What are you hoping to investigate further? Remember that the people running your course care *so much* about the subject and will be salivating at the thought of someone excited to scuba-dive into it. For top universities, I'd recommend taking this one step further and making your statement at least 80 per cent academic, if not more. Also, if things haven't gone to plan in the past – for example, if your GCSE results weren't *quite* what you'd hoped for – this could be a great place to explain why this was the case, and, most importantly, how you've developed since.

3. **How to talk about extra-curricular activities:** Okay, so you play for a hockey team, have a bronze Duke of Edinburgh Award and used to babysit your neighbour's cat once a month, but does that really make a university want you? The answer isn't actually a

14

straightforward no. You can use all of these things to your advantage by linking them back to your degree. As an example, I used the final paragraph of my personal statement to share some extra-curricular activities I'd partaken in, which could be utilised to prove my interest in the subject and assimilated with the rest of the essay, rather than being slapped on at the end. This section should be like the air freshener placed in your vehicle after a car wash, tying the whole thing together and packing that final citrusy punch. For example, when applying for an English Literature degree, I chose to focus on the use of language in novels, particularly psychoanalytical and feminist ones. Then, when I spoke about my extra-curriculars, I continued to discuss language, explaining how I had to alter my word choices, tone and sentence structure when addressing the children in the library I volunteered at, my peers in my role as Head Boy of my school and the audience of my online blog. When I played for a football team for ten years, I communicated with my teammates in a very different way to how I addressed customers in my part-time retail job. This was essentially a bedazzled list of my interests and achievements outside of the education system, adorned with references back to my interest in the subject I wished to study. Always, always, always link it back to the degree!

4. **Referencing texts:** Your personal statement should absolutely, definitely reference several texts outside of the standard curriculum, which prove that you are an *active* student. What I mean by the word *active* is that you are engaged, astute and interested in that area of study: if you're hungry to learn more, then you're the perfect university candidate, right? Making reference to texts you have explored in your own time is absolutely vital – it's called a *personal* statement because it's about your personal passion for the subject. Also, texts don't have to be books; they can be podcasts, TED talks, films, articles, blog posts or even songs. The more unique, the better. Also, don't assume that academics are snobby about what texts you reference – as long as they're utilised in the correct context, and balanced by scholarly material, they're valid and relevant. Be careful not to simply reel off texts, though. You're better off writing about a limited number of texts than sending off a shopping list disguised as a bibliography. Maybe focus on one or two primary texts, then refer to critical material surrounding it, and discuss your opinions and thoughts, as well as what you'd be interested to investigate further if given the opportunity. Hey – that opportunity could be going to the university! What a startling coincidence! Cut to the admissions officer rubbing their hands together in glee.

5. **Actually read the texts you reference:** You'd have thought this would be obvious, right? Still, it definitely needs saying. Don't mention anything you haven't genuinely listened to, watched or read, because you'll only make yourself look more foolish than if you'd referenced nothing at all. It'll shine like a strobe light in a nightclub if you haven't *actually* done the work you're claiming. Allow me to share a personal, rather traumatic, anecdote that should hammer this into your head. So, in my personal statement, I mentioned Nabokov's novel *Lolita*. When I had an interview at Oxford University, the professor conducting the interview said to me that he had noticed this in my personal statement, since *Lolita* was a novel he had dedicated his life's research to, and Nabokov was an author he specialised in and lectured on as a scholar. He proceeded to open the (conveniently placed) drawer of his desk and pull out his very own copy, which had – I am absolutely certain – been placed there specifically in anticipation of my interview for dramatic effect. He looked me in the eye and, with a smirk, asked 'How does it begin?' My heart racing like Mo Farah and my mind frantically rummaging through the filing cabinets of memories in my brain, I desperately tried to recall the opening scene of a novel I'd read years ago by the pool on holiday in Majorca. Thankfully, I *had* read the novel and did manage to recall the first scene, but if I had only read a SparkNotes

overview, I would've been well and truly screwed. That was nearly a horror story the *Saw* franchise would've been proud of and was only narrowly averted. YOU HAVE TO READ THE BOOKS YOU REFERENCE.

6. **This is a No-B.S. zone:** Avoid exaggeration and hyperbole, and be realistic. So many people naturally feel the urge to open their personal statements by suggesting that the genesis of their interest in Biology was the moment they were plucked from the womb, screaming and crying only because they were so ecstatic to be entering a world where they would eventually have the opportunity to study this subject at university. By saying, 'I've always had an interest in biology,' you're not really saying anything at all. It's also just not true. I'm sure you didn't give a toss about the structure of a leaf or the process of osmosis when you were three years old and needed assistance zipping up your own raincoat. Instead of declaring that you've *always* possessed a passion for ~~fashion~~ Biology, talk about why you're fascinated by it *now*.

7. **Link your degree to the other subjects you studied:** Just because you aren't taking your other A Level subjects further, it doesn't mean the insight they gave you won't be valuable to your degree. So, if you're applying to a Geography degree but also took Politics at A Level, you could make your personal statement

more interesting by focusing on a geopolitical discussion – a perfect fusion of the two. If you also took psychology, you could go on to discuss this in relation to the other two subjects as well, but always link back to the course you're actually applying to study as the main emphasis. You don't have to do this, but it might be a good starting point when you embark on the odyssey that is writing a personal statement.

8. **How do you begin a personal statement?**
Unfortunately, I don't have a straightforward answer to this question, because the personal statement is unique to every single person. The opening line should definitely be eye-catching, to make the admissions officer – who, by the way, is probably on personal statement 104 of the day – immediately want you. Some people opt for a quote, while others pose a question, but the important thing is to then expand on this and keep drawing back to it. Don't just chuck it in for the sake of it, because it'll be startlingly obvious if that's what you've done.

9. **Don't expect it to be perfect straight away.** Just like any essay, the personal statement takes time. Except, in this case, you've never written a personal statement before, or been able to practise and hone your craft. Draft and re-draft ... then re-draft again. Get feedback from subject-specific teachers. Ask your parents to read it to make sure it's coherent and makes sense on a fundamental level. Get your peers to read it, too. And, most importantly, don't be too protective over it. The first draft won't be perfect, and all the feedback you receive will be completely invaluable. Don't be offended if someone says they don't understand, or if a teacher tells you that what you're saying isn't accurate – take it on the chin and see how you can improve what you've written. It'll come together eventually, but don't expect to master it straight away.

The extras

Not sure how to prove that you're the perfect candidate? I get it; it's difficult to prove your interest in a subject, and most of us are unlikely to have dedicated much time to it outside of school, because we're too busy focusing on – well – school. Here are some ideas on how to improve your application right now:

- *Look for articles online (for example on JSTOR and Google Scholar). To go deeper, or find something more appropriate, check the bibliography of an article as these can be gold mines for more refined essays that you didn't spot on first inspection.*

- *Start a blog/podcast that discusses the subject. You don't have to share this with anyone you know and can keep it totally anonymous. It just proves you have an organic interest in the subject, which you want to discuss and share. The easiest way to start a blog is by using WordPress.com.*

- *Search for some TED talks on the subject area. They're short and concise but also investigate a complex idea in some depth. They're also usually pretty easy to understand so (hopefully) won't take too much deciphering!*

- *Ask your teachers for recommendations. They'll be able to guide you towards something they know you'll find interesting that isn't on the curriculum – remember, they've probably got a degree in the subject themselves!*

- *Prove your interest in the subject by doing an EPQ (Extended Project Qualification)! Some universities will lower your grade entry requirements if you do well in your EPQ, but others will just take it as confirmation that you are an active researcher of the subject you have chosen. This could also be a great opportunity to combine your interest in your different A Level subjects, by writing an essay that incorporates all of them to some degree.*

10 tips to ace your A Levels

Before you go to university, you've got to earn your place there, and it'll probably be one of the most intense periods of study you'll ever have to endure. However, there is a light at the end of the tunnel, and that light looks like a three-month summer and a whole lot of celebrating, so hang on in there. With a bit of determination and dedication, there's nothing stopping you from achieving those grades, so put in the work today and you'll be thanking yourself when you arrive at your dream uni in Freshers' Week. Here are 10 things you can start doing right now to boost your grades …

1. **Plan Your Revision:** I used to make a timetable at the start of each day, which broke the time down into 15-minute slots. That way, I knew exactly what I needed to be doing and when – the more specific, the better. Examples would be spending 45 minutes making flash cards about DNA for Biology, then an hour making mind maps about each character in a book you're studying for English, then 15 minutes spent going back over the flash cards you made on DNA. That's two hours of focused work with specific goals that you can tick off. My plans always had columns for the time and the activity, and then a tick box. Ticking things off makes me feel so much more productive somewhere in my brain and motivates me to keep

22

working and ticking away like a clock. Make sure you also tick off things like breaks, having breakfast or even just dragging yourself out of bed, because those are vital as well. Being productive doesn't always mean working yourself to exhaustion – it means working yourself efficiently and effectively. With this in mind, also be realistic. For instance, if you get home from school at 4 p.m., you're not very likely to want to start studying straight away, so give yourself some time to just chill.

2. **Plan Your Answers:** For written answers, which occur in pretty much every subject in some capacity (including more sciencey subjects), planning your essay or answer in advance will make it so much more concise, accurate and coherent. Before exam season rears its ugly head, make essay plans or check past papers to see what wording is always referenced, and mirror it in your answers. Mark schemes for subjects like Biology, Chemistry and Physics are usually looking for you to reference very specific words and specialist vocabulary, so practise using them and plan your potential answers. For humanities subjects, making practice essay plans for potential questions makes you realise where the gaps in your knowledge are, and can help perfect the structure of your arguments. Also, write out a basic version of the plan on your exam paper and keep referring back to it as you answer the

question. I remember my history teacher (who was an exam marker) saying that whenever she opened the exam paper of a random candidate and saw a plan, it made her instantly think that person was organised, well prepared and focused. So psychologically she was already *expecting* the answer to be good. This could really work in your favour and wow the examiner straight off the bat. Honestly, just trick them into thinking you're clever.

3. **Set Short-term Goals:** Having the goal of 'revise for this exam' is great, but you can break that down much, much further. Grab an A4 sheet of paper and bullet point a list of all the things you want to do before that exam to revise for it, being as specific as possible (make mind maps on the process of mitosis; create flash cards to make sure I remember the names of each step; draw a big diagram so I can visually remember it, etc.). Instead of saying 'make notes from the textbook', divide up the book into blocks of 10 pages, so every time you make notes on a set of 10 pages you feel like you've actually achieved something. It's like building a skyscraper and feeling a sense of accomplishment for each new floor that is built, rather than only celebrating once it's 500 metres tall. I also find it useful to focus on individual topics for a week at a time, so that I *really* focus on them, instead of having my finger in more pies than Paul Hollywood.

4. **Block Your Distractions:** You're not a revision robot who can just turn on 'focus mode' like Buzz Lightyear's Spanish setting – you're a human being. So, realistically, distractions will arise. However, there are ways of preventing this. There's a phone app called Forest, which grows a tree for the amount of time you're aiming to study for, and if you use your phone during that time then it kills off the tree. This sounds silly, but, trust me, it's tree-mendous. Alternatively, there's an application you can download to your computer called Self Control, which blacklists websites for a set time period – meaning you won't even be able to load up social-media sites. If you can't stop playing your Xbox, give your parents the remote and tell them you're going to revise – because the pain of having to admit that you've been defeated by temptation and want the controller back will be far worse than just doing the revision. I definitely believe in the maxim 'Out of sight, out of mind', so if my phone is physically far away from me (my most common hiding spot is inside a box of cereal) then the effort of going all the way downstairs to retrieve it just to check my Instagram feed (which always turns into at least half an hour of mindless scrolling) just isn't worth it.

5. **Condense and Condense Again:** Create your own revision resource by condensing down all your research and notes into your own folders or notepads,

and then condense that down again into just the vital information you need to memorise. One thing I did that really helped me out was to make an 'information bank' – and this can be used for most subjects. This breaks down a whole textbook into just the vital bits you need to lodge into your brain and makes it all feel a lot more manageable. This technique is particularly good for exams that require you to learn quotes or case studies, such as Law, Politics, Psychology or English. I'd create a table on a Word document, which has different columns with the headings: Source/Person, Quote/Idea, Theme and Analysis. Always make sure you add in that section at the end for analysis, so you're constantly encouraging yourself to think critically, as this is what will boost you into the top tier of grades. Then, turn these crucial bits of info into flash cards, index cards and mind maps to help you remember them.

6. **Efficient Revision Is More Important than Time Spent Revising:** Why spend two hours reading from a textbook, when you could spend 30 minutes making, and then revising from, flash cards? The latter will be so much more productive and time efficient, and your brain will be much more active – and therefore more likely to absorb the information rather than merely skimming over a black hole of words. One way to use flash cards effectively is to sort them out into different piles, depending on how well you know them. Initially

all of them start in a 'revise every day' pile. If there are flash cards that you're consistently answering correctly, they move up into a 'revise every other day' pile. If you're getting them right every other day, they move up into 'revise once a week', and then eventually 'revise the night before the exam'. If you get a flash card wrong – even once – move it all the way back to the beginning, so you're revising it every day again. This means you're spending more time focusing on the things that aren't quite sticking, rather than wasting time going over flash cards you know like the back of your hand. Work smarter, not harder.

7. **Not Everything Has to Be Neat:** As a self-confessed 'neat freak', I know full well how many of us like to have our revision notes looking tidy. However, let that go for a minute, because it could be tripping you up and causing you to land with your face in the dirt. And that dirt looks very much like 'not knowing the answers in the exam'. Get a blank scrap of paper, make a mind map, pick a subject, and then just scrawl everything you know about that topic. Draw arrows, make connections, make it scruffy, and give yourself time to just *think*. Eventually, everything will click into your brain. In your exam you need to be critical and analytical, identifying connections and contrasts between ideas – so practise it now! Once you've had this initial brain dump, make a neat version where you

consolidate everything. Just call yourself Hannah Montana, because you've got the best of both worlds, my friend.

8. **Find Your Study Space:** I know for a fact that I can't work in my room because I'm just not as efficient or productive there. Instead, I use local libraries because I like to work in silence to really focus, but a lot of my friends find the buzz of a café a healthy working environment, too. Working in a location where lots of other people are studying is incredibly conducive, because the general atmosphere of hard work all around you encourages you to do the same. Even the act of leaving the house and *going* somewhere to revise gives you purpose, and once you've put in that amount of effort, you might as well put in the work to make it worthwhile.

9. **Teach Yourself as You Go:** The main difference between my first and second year of sixth form – aside from slightly more facial hair and a lot less sleep – was that I did a lot more independent learning and research in my second year. Your school will probably have ample resources both in their library and online, but I'd particularly recommend the 'review' journals (*Geography Review, Physics Review, Politics Review*, etc.), which are specifically targeted at an A Level-student audience. Check out local libraries, or request

that your school subscribes to these magazines, as they'll be super useful. Also, when you do this work, make notes on it for future reference. Even though you *think* you will, you won't remember everything you read, so make bullet-pointed lists to refer back to. Not only will this improve your time in lessons because you'll have interesting thoughts or opinions to share, but it'll also be incredibly helpful and time efficient when exam season comes over the hill.

10. **Look After Yourself:** You need to make sure that *you're* doing okay before you even think about pushing yourself to work for another hour. Your life doesn't have to stop just because of exam season, so take time out for yourself and continue doing the things you love. Running, climbing or swimming are great because time spent doing those activities is time where your brain is completely focused on something outside of revision. Take days off, and don't push yourself to the point of burnout – because that's actually less productive, even if you are spending hours slaving over your laptop. Work hard, yes, but look after yourself, too. You've got this and it'll all be over soon, I promise. Good luck!

Preparing for results day

Judgment Day is here, and it's time to face the music. Lots of people will tell you to bubble-wrap yourself in positive energy and soak yourself in *good vibes* because '*don't worry, there's nothing you can do about it now*' – like, yes, Karen, I know that … and the fact that I can't do anything about it is what's freaking me out.

If you, like me, find results day very daunting and intimidating, then you've probably got your excuses in early: I accidentally wrote my paper in blue ink so they refused to mark it; oops, I wrote someone else's name and candidate number; maybe someone copied my *correct* answers and we both got disqualified …? Either that, or you're going to attempt to convince your parents that D stands for 'Definitely have a bright future ahead of you', F stands for 'Future looks bright' and U stands for 'University is your next step'.

So here, I want to give you some more practical tips about preparing for results day, and to have a proper, honest chat about it.

First and foremost, it's important to remember that no matter what happens or what numbers are printed on that sheet of A4 paper, you have achieved something. You have survived a really difficult, mentally taxing year and made it to this point. You have *achieved* your grades and the qualifications they provide you with. Don't you dare forget that.

The thing about results day is that it's really just results morning – or results five minutes if all goes to plan. However, there's a lot of horrible anticipation in the build-up, so I think it's important to make sure you have a good plan for the day. Organise to meet with friends in the evening or do something with your family, so you have plans you can actually look forward to. Also, don't cut out your normal habits just because results day is happening – give yourself a sense of normality by keeping your routine as ordinary as you can. Have the same breakfast you'd normally eat, go to bed at your usual time the night before. Give yourself some sense of normality among the chaos.

Think about what grades you will be satisfied with, because ultimately this day is about you and no one else. Social media will always be saturated with success stories, and there's always that one pair of gleaming twins on *BBC Breakfast* who have somehow done seven A Levels each and got A*s in all of them. Make sure you know what you're hoping for, and what you'll be pleased with before celebratory Instagram posts start to litter your timeline. It's not about what your best friend got, or what your older siblings got, or what your mum's cousin's hamster's previous owner's son-in-law got. It's about you.

Also, be mindful. What you might consider a 'fail' or a bad mark could be someone else's dream grade. Everyone is on their own path and striving for their own goals, so there's no need for comparison. Focus on yourself, and let others do the same.

One thing I would recommend is conjuring up a contingency plan. I know it sounds a bit like tempting fate, but I'd really recommend making an account on the UCAS Clearing page, downloading the Clearing app and writing down the phone numbers for your prospective university's admissions office. You don't want to be frantically googling alternatives at 9.05 a.m. after the results come out, so make sure you know who you need to contact if anything goes slightly awry.

Equally, make sure you know what your alternatives are. Could you retake your exams and defer your application? Would you be interested in taking a gap year and reapplying next year once you know what grades you're working with? Would your skills be best utilised in a more practical environment? Now is the time to think about it!

Maybe you'll find that you actually did really well in a subject you weren't expecting. Know that results day isn't too late to have a change of heart and change universities or even courses. One of my friends decided to change what degree she was going to study, from economics to fashion, and has been thriving on her course ever since. You've got to make sure you're doing what makes *you* happy and utilising your unique skillset.

When it comes to opening the envelope of terror, make sure you open it in an environment you feel comfortable in, among people you feel comfortable with. Have a good support system around you, where there's no sense of competition, guilt or unwarranted stress.

Above all, good luck! I hope results day goes exactly the way you're hoping it will, and if not, then I promise everything will fall into place for you eventually. I've got everything crossed for you.

Dealing with rejection (spoiler alert: it's going to be okay)

One of life's cruellest lessons is that sometimes not everything works out in the picture-perfect way you planned in your head. Not everyone will recognise the potential you know you have, the commitment and dedication you know you can provide, or the gift you know you possess. And that's tough, even heartbreaking, so let's not pretend for another second that it isn't.

When I was rejected by my dream university, I collapsed into myself, like a wilting flower or an expectant hand recoiling after someone aired my high-five. I felt like a failure, like I'd let everyone around me down, that I'd embarrassed myself for even trying. That I *deserved* rejection, or that karma was finally coming to bite me in the arse for not forwarding on that chainmail in 2011. I had it coming, right? I needed a reason, or an excuse, and couldn't find one that existed outside of the four walls of my own capabilities. So I just deflated like a balloon and wallowed in a swamp of self-pity and introspection, feeling stupid, hopeless and just a bit silly, really. But then I decided that I had to be okay. Because there was no other option.

Before you do that, however, allow yourself to feel the pain – and *really* feel it. Experience it. Understand it. Don't blame yourself for being susceptible to human emotions, and give

34

yourself time to come to terms with it. Rejection can feel like a loss in some ways, because it's a specific door closing, and probably one you'd hoped would be held open for you. Just think of the phrases we use to describe rejection: a kick in the teeth; a slap in the face; a serious blow; a punch in the gut. All these idioms and platitudes liken the sensation of rejection to physical pain, because that is how humans respond to it. It's normal, and it's okay.

In fact, Guy Winch's book *Emotional First Aid* reports that rejection is such a strong emotion that the body registers the sensation as if it *were* physical pain. Brain scans have revealed that the two sensations even manifest themselves in identical regions of the brain, and so rejection rears its ugly head in both a visceral and physical way. In a ball-tossing experiment depicted in Winch's study, three strangers in a waiting room start throwing a ball among themselves, until one is deliberately excluded from the game by the other players, who were really just (evil) scientists in disguise. The person who found themselves in an unwitting game of piggy-in-the-middle reported feeling deep pain at the moment of recognition that they had been rejected by the others. Those given Tylenol (a pain-relief drug) experienced this feeling to a lesser extent, and yet the drug was ineffective at relieving other emotions like embarrassment. Rejection *is* like a physical pain, and if there are people in lab coats backing up that claim then I'm not here to question it.

The point is this: rejection appears to be the most ostensible manifestation of failure in our lives, and it really doesn't discriminate. No one gets a get-out-of-jail-free card, and yet there's no way of preparing for it or softening the blow. But rejection isn't the end of the road, and it's certainly not one big epic fail. Rejection is redirection, and a route to different opportunities. It's a chance to have a fresh start, to re-evaluate and come back stronger. Learn from it, take it on the chin and improve. Know more next time.

Also, don't take rejection too personally. Remember that what one person perceives as your 'weakness', another person will deem to be your greatest strength. When Anna Wintour was fired from a magazine job because the editor at the time thought her shoots were too edgy, that editor didn't know that she'd later be crossing her fingers for Wintour, now editor-in-chief of American *Vogue*, to bless her with a Met Gala invite. When Oprah Winfrey was fired from a Baltimore broadcaster for being too empathetic and emotionally involved with her interviewees, she didn't know that this perceived 'weakness' would later make her a billionaire. When U2 were declined by RSO Records, they never would've believed they could go on to sell 170 million records worldwide, or have the heaviest mantelpiece *ever*, since it's decorated with 22 Grammys.

For most of us, minor rejections probably won't lead to 14 studio albums, but that's beside the point. The true tragedy would be to give up trying, or to crumble entirely and let the rejection overwhelm us or make us settle for less. Being rejected from my 'dream' university led me down a different path, to a different university and a different experience. To a place which has allowed me to thrive. To a university I now adore. In fact, this book wouldn't exist without that rejection, and I can honestly say that if Doctor Who appeared in the TARDIS right now with the offer to go back in time and change it all, I'd let time play out in exactly the way it did. Because I'm better for it. Because I needed rejection to be where I am now. (Although I would still take up the opportunity to have a ride in the TARDIS and maybe give Henry VIII's wives the heads-up.*)

Rejection will happen in our lives, and that's okay. In fact, in a weird, twisted, messed-up kind of way, it's necessary.

That said, in the context of applying to university (that's what this book is all about, after all), don't let fear of rejection stop you from applying to the places you dream of. They may feel unattainable or impossible, but if you never try, you'll never know. It's important to remember that there are *always* options, be it Clearing,** Adjustment,*** a gap year or second choices, so you'll be all right. Keep pushing and remember who you are. You'll thank yourself in six months' time.

Now you've accepted and embraced it, it's time to dust yourself off, reset and come back stronger. Time to prove 'em

---

* Giving Henry VIII's wives the *heads-up* is probably the most insensitive use of the English language ever, since two of them were literally beheaded. Sorry about that, Anne and Cath.

** Clearing is the process by which you can still go to university, even if you didn't meet the offer your firm-choice university gave you.

*** Adjustment is essentially the opposite of Clearing: when you do *better* than you expected to, and move to a university with higher entry requirements.

wrong and become one of those success stories we spoke about earlier.

CHAPTER 2

SO YOU'RE OFF TO UNIVERSITY ...

You've done it – congratulations! I hope you're buzzing and celebrating irresponsibly. Now that you've met your offer and got your place, the excitement can really begin. But how on earth do you prepare for such a life-changing moment? Here are a few pointers ...

What to pack

Here's a checklist of all the essentials you'll need to take to university with you. No matter how much you prepare and attempt to streamline the process, I can absolutely guarantee that you will a) end up with a FULL car and have to carry everything into your new room looking like a human Buckaroo, and b) inevitably forget *something*. Hopefully this will help you keep track of what you've got! There are two boxes next to each item, so you can tick them off when you've bought it and when you've packed it.

One tip I would add to the 'Kitchen' section is to check with your housemates* (if you can) before moving in what utensils they're bringing. For example, there's no real need for a house of 10 people to have 10 cheese graters. Although that'd still be better than paying an exorbitant price for supermarket pre-grated cheese. It's time to make Britain *grate* again.

Kitchen

- Cutlery ☐ ☐
- Plates and bowls ☐ ☐
- Glasses ☐ ☐
- Pots and pans ☐ ☐

---

* Let's call them housemates regardless of whether you're sharing a house, a flat, a dorm or a halls-of-residence corridor – it makes life simpler.

- Wooden spoon ☐ ☐
- Spatula ☐ ☐
- Tea towels ☐ ☐
- Colander ☐ ☐
- Kettle ☐ ☐
- Toaster ☐ ☐
- Oven mitts ☐ ☐
- Knives ☐ ☐
- Bottle opener and corkscrew ☐ ☐
- Chopping board ☐ ☐
- Cheese grater ☐ ☐

Most kitchen stuff can be cheaply acquired from charity shops.

Remember, just because IKEA sells a very specific kitchen gadget, that doesn't mean you need it in your uni kitchen.

Bedroom

- Pillows and duvet ☐ ☐
- Mattress topper ☐ ☐
- Bed linen and pillowcases ☐ ☐
- Cushions and a throw ☐ ☐
  This is a good way of getting a bit of a colour scheme going and making your uni room really cosy and unique.

- Desk/bedside lamp ☐ ☐
- Fairy lights ☐ ☐
- Alarm clock. ☐ ☐
  Those 9 a.m. lectures are going to go ahead with
  or without you.
- Towels ☐ ☐
- Shower caddy ☐ ☐
- Whiteboard for notes ☐ ☐
- Laundry basket/bag ☐ ☐
  The ones that have separate compartments for
  lights/darks/colours are particularly good, as this
  will save you a job and hopefully prevent a rogue
  red sock from turning your entire wardrobe
  magenta.
- Posters and photos ☐ ☐
  Another good way to distract from the dull dorm
  walls as much as possible.
- Houseplants ☐ ☐
  Lots of university cities have houseplant sales in
  the first couple of weeks to help you stock up,
  and local markets are great, too. Alternatively, if
  you're struggling to keep yourself alive and you're
  not sure you can extend your efforts to another
  living organism, maybe invest in a fake plant ...
- Hangers ☐ ☐

Stationery

- Pens (black and coloured) and pencils ☐ ☐
- (Clear) pencil case ☐ ☐
- Stapler ☐ ☐
- Rucksack ☐ ☐
- Highlighters ☐ ☐
- Folders and dividers ☐ ☐

    Get into a routine where you file away all your loose paperwork and lecture handouts once a fortnight. Stick on a TV show or film and fill up your folders!

- Paper clips ☐ ☐
- Notepads ☐ ☐
- Index cards/flash cards ☐ ☐
- Noticeboard pins ☐ ☐

    Most uni dorms will have a noticeboard on the wall for you to use.

- Hole punch

Storage

- Baskets ☐ ☐
- Boxes ☐ ☐
- Over-door hook ☐ ☐

    This keeps your towels (and dressing gown) off the floor and makes them easy to hang to dry. I'd also recommend having an umbrella hanging there, too ... for keeping you dry, not the towels.

- Tupperware
  *Ohana means family, and family means no
  food gets left behind.*
- Suitcase
- Pen pot

Miscellaneous

- Laptop
- Chargers
- Playing cards
- Extension lead(s)
- Air freshener (!!!) – seriously.
- Clubbing shoes
  *If there's one thing I've learnt at university, it's that
  student clubs are grim. They're where your fresh
  new trainers go to die, and the floors are so sticky
  the glue-stick in your pencil case will be jealous.
  Bring an old tatty pair of trainers which you don't
  mind getting mucky, or purchase some from a
  charity shop ... you won't regret it.*
- Slippers
- Doorstop
  *It's a good idea to wedge your door open during
  Freshers' Week, especially on move-in day, so
  that people can chat to you whenever they want.
  It makes you seem warm and inviting, and saves
  the awkwardness of having to knock on your new
  housemate's door to say hey.*

45

- Key hook □ □
  I'm sure you'll become well acquainted with the porter or receptionist of your halls of residence when you inevitably get locked out, but at least a key hook will show that you tried.
- Command strips □ □
  Adhesive strips for sticking things to the wall (think posters, picture frames, fairy lights, etc.), which don't leave any damage.
- Academic planner □ □
- Copies of important documents – you never know when you'll need them! □ □
- Ear plugs. University walls are thin. So very thin. □ □
- Spare batteries □ □
- Speaker □ □
- Hard drive □ □
  Make sure your stuff is all backed up! If you don't want to spend money on a physical hard drive, make sure your documents are saved to Google Drive or something similar.

How much should I read before term begins?

Ahhhh, the age-old question. You're about to embark on your university odyssey and you can't wait for Freshers' Week, but the huge workload is breathing down your neck like an over-zealous waiter 45 seconds after giving you a menu.

Well, the first thing I'd say is **don't panic** – you'll be fine regardless of how much (or how little) you know or have read before the course starts. If they were expecting you to be the finished product, you'd have your graduation cap already adorning your head, and a lifetime of debt already acquired. You don't ... yet. And that's fine.

There will always be those who seem to know absolutely everything there is to know about the course, to the point where you wonder whether the person you just introduced yourself to outside the lecture theatre is actually the lecturer themselves in disguise, trying to root out the weakest links, Anne Robinson-style. They're not – unless your lecturer is a sadist, which I can't guarantee. These people are just trying to intimidate you with their supposed wisdom. They may know the first 38 digits of pi, or the capital city of every country in Europe, but they're sitting in exactly the same lectures as you and have just as much of a chance of succeeding. Plus, the best thing about uni grading is that there's no quota of different grades or bell-diagram to emulate. Theoretically, everyone could get a First. So good luck to Mr or Mrs Show-off – we hope you do well ... ish.

What I'm trying to say is that you earned your place on the course just as much as anyone else did, so focus on yourself and what you know, rather than what everyone else seems to. The thing about university subjects is that they're broad and expansive,* yet have an infinite number of specialisations. That means your research and reading will lead you in completely different directions – and to completely different answers – to everyone around you.

Over the summer, in an ideal world, you should focus on the first few weeks of reading material. In particular, try to do the first one or two weeks of reading, as Freshers' Week will be pretty chaotic, leaving limited opportunities to actually focus on work, whether you want or (most likely) don't want to do it. Further, the emotional and physical intensity of Freshers' Week will inevitably leave you shattered like glass near an opera singer, so any work you can do in advance will allow you to completely unwind. Basically, do something today that your future self will thank you for. Yep, that's a quote that should be etched into a plank of wood for mums across the country to put up in their living rooms.

If you are ahead of the game and do manage to get the preliminary weeks' reading done, do yourself a favour and read

---

* This says expansive, but if you accidentally read the line as 'The thing about university subjects is that they're broad and expEnsive', that's still pretty accurate.

the work set for the last two weeks of first term as well, because by that point you'll be exhausted, drowning in a sea of deadlines and viewing the Christmas break as a kind of rehab. Trust me, you'll really appreciate being on top of things at that point.

Try to remember that any prep work you do at university (be it for lectures, tutorials or seminars) will only put you at an advantage when it comes to essays, presentations, assignments and, ultimately, exams. The more research you do before a contact hour with an academic, the more you'll gain from it, so see it as an advantage rather than something that should be dreaded at the start of term as a form of contraception against having fun.

The university dictionary

All the university jargon you'll hear on a daily basis, compiled into one handy guide ...

Academic advisor: An academic who is assigned to you at the beginning of your first year. They schedule meetings with you to check up on your progress and should be your first port of call when you need advice.

Alumni: Past students who have graduated from the university (usually called upon by said university when the uni is in need of some money).

BA: A Bachelor of Arts or, in my opinion, a long-term investment into having a personality.

BSc: A Bachelor of Science (think Chemistry, Physics, Biology, Maths, etc.) or, in my opinion, a long-term investment into having dispoable income.

Bursary: A grant awarded to someone (for example, for academic achievement).

Ball: A big ol' party, which often involves a fancy dress code, a fancy meal and some less-than-fancy behaviour.

College: Some universities are sub-divided into colleges, which are basically just student communities and somewhere to live in first year. It's also what Americans call university for no apparent reason, but then again, they call courgettes zucchini and knock about with guns, so I don't necessarily hold the US as the cornerstone of all wisdom ...

Combined Honours: When you take two subjects together at university because you're spoilt for choice.

Degree: I'm not 100 per cent sure – will get back to you on this one.

Department: Different subject areas within the university (e.g. the Maths Department).

Dissertation: The much-dreaded, roughly 10,000–12,000-word essay written in your final year (or, in most cases, in the 10 days before the deadline).

Dorm: Your bedroom at university, probably decorated with empty vodka bottles and beer cans.

Finalist: Someone in their final year at university, or a contestant who got past Judges' Houses on *The X Factor*.

Fresher: A first-year student (often referred to as 'silly fresh').

Freshers' Flu: The inevitable, seemingly life-threatening illness every student magically gets (no matter which year you're in) by week three of first term.

Freshers' Week: Your first week at university, full of partying, socialising and regret.

Gap yah student: The student who's a year older because they went travelling. Often identifiable by the tapestry on their wall, the 'throwback' pictures on their Instagram and the tattoos on their arms. DID I MENTION THEY WENT TRAVELLING?

Graduand: Someone who has finished their course but hasn't yet had their graduation ceremony – basically just a good word for the CV when you're not *officially* a graduate.

Graduate: Someone who has completed their degree and has the certificate to prove it.

Graduation: The ceremony where you are awarded a certificate, crying parents and a new Facebook profile picture.

Halls of residence: Where you are assigned to live in your first year of university among fellow students ... aka the most chaotic place to ever exist.

Honours degree: A degree with 'honours' basically just means that instead of a simple pass or fail, there's a gradation of achievement (i.e. 1st, 2:1, 2:2, etc.) – so the 'honours' bit is basically how well you did.

Initiation: Often disguised these days as 'welcome drinks', this will be your enrolment into the social side of university clubs and societies.

International student: Easily the best-dressed people on campus, international students come from abroad to study in the UK.

Lecture: When an academic presents an hour-long talk on a specific topic, without interruption (seriously – don't be that person who interrupts a lecturer).

Lecturer: Someone who knows enough about a topic to talk about it for a whole hour and still somehow sound smart.

MA: Master of Art (postgraduate study for people who are either super-keen or just don't want to grow up yet and will do anything to put off being a proper adult).

Matriculation: A welcome ceremony that some universities (like Oxford, Cambridge and Durham) hold in your first week, to mark your official enrolment in the university.

MSc: Master of Science (postgraduate study for people who are both super-keen *and* don't want to grow up yet).

Office hours: Each member of academic staff has 'office hours' – when they will be free for you to go and hound them with questions. Take advantage of this!

Plagiarism: When you copy the work or ideas from another person, and most likely get penalised for it. You will be caught for doing this, so don't.

Postgrad: Someone who has already got a degree, but has come back for more.

Seminar: A mix between a lecture and a tutorial, usually with about double the number of people as a tutorial, but with a combination of teaching and discussion.

Sharking: When someone who is not a fresher gets with a fresher. SHARK BAIT HOO-HA-HA. Imagine the *Jaws* music playing as they approach you.

Tutorial: A small teaching class, where you are often expected to do some research, prepare some work, do a presentation or answer questions. Usually there are between one and eight people in a tutorial, alongside an academic who leads the session.

Tutor: Leads your tutorials and sets your essays.

Undergrad: Someone who hasn't yet got their degree but is working on it.

Vice-chancellor: The person in charge of the university, usually with a yearly salary that more closely resembles a phone number than a pay check.

Freshers' Week

Let's talk about Freshers' Week

So … it's Freshers' Week: time to let your hair – and your family – down. What will probably be one of the busiest, craziest, maybe even scariest weeks of your life is about to start, and that's exciting, overwhelming and confusing all at the same time. You'll find yourself totally drained in approximately three to five working days, and with a throat that croaks like a frog. Yep, Freshers' Flu is real. It won't be pretty, but it'll be worth it, as you'll most likely have such a whale of a time you'll give Moby Dick a run for its money.

This is a fantastic opportunity that you're so lucky to have, and your first chance to take university life by the teats and milk it. Be yourself, get stuck in and set yourself up for all the experiences you hoped university would bring. But also look after yourself … you've got this.

Should you buy Freshers' tickets before uni?

Probably not. This is a prime opportunity for scamming impressionable Freshers who believe it when a club which doesn't actually exist says online that it's THE ULTIMATE FRESHERS' WELCOME PARTY – NOT TO BE MISSED *ONLY 5 TICKETS REMAINING*.

Unless the Students' Union (SU) or your accommodation providers specifically tell you to buy a 'Freshers' wristband', I probably wouldn't risk it. If in doubt, message the SU for your uni and they'll give you the advice you need.

(Please note: This advice is coming from *that* idiot who paid £10 for THE OFFICIAL FRESHERS' OPENING NIGHT, only to find out that the nightclub it was being hosted in didn't exist, and by the time Freshers' Week rolled around the website I'd bought it from had disappeared. I've got 'mug' written on my forehead.)

Top Freshers' Week tips

1. Go to the Freshers' Fair and join as many clubs and societies as you're interested in (see 'Clubs and societies', page 159). Go to taster sessions if possible to get a feel for all the different things you can do in your time at uni. This is the best way to meet like-minded people, learn new skills and enjoy improving your old ones.

2. Say hello to everyone. Believe me when I say that the person you feel too awkward to introduce yourself to is feeling the exact same way, so make the first move. Everyone is in the same boat, in a strange place surrounded by strange people, and the questions just write themselves: What's your name? What course are

you doing? Where are you from?* Do you know anyone else at the uni? Do you play any sports? How has your week been so far? Have you had any cooking disasters yet? What are your housemates like? What's your accommodation like? What's your name again because I've already forgotten it? You'll never have another opportunity like this where it *isn't* weird to just go and say hey to complete strangers all the time. You really have nothing to lose.

3. Embrace the freebies. Companies, clubs, societies, departments, etc., will be *throwing* freebies at you like confetti during Freshers' Week, from restaurant discounts and sweet treats to free wall planners and water bottles. Take what you can get, because if there's one thing students love, it's a freebie. You might as well get your money's worth out of that uni.

4. Most universities will have houseplant sales and poster sales in the first couple of weeks, and these are quite inexpensive ways of making your dorm room your own and breathing some life into it. Deck the halls.

---

* Prepare yourself to realise that your geographical knowledge of the UK is absolutely abysmal. Also, get used to having your accent mocked by pretty much anyone who isn't from the same place as you. The North/South divide is real. If you're from the Midlands, pick a side.

5. Hang out with your housemates, and make sure you have some proper bonding time as a house/flat. My housemates and I quickly realised that we were all avid fans of *The Great British Bake Off* (then again, who isn't?) and so made a plan to all have dinner together on the third night of Freshers' Week and watch an episode. We also made a cleaning rota, as well as a birthday board so we knew when (and who) to celebrate. This was such an easy ice-breaker and made us all instantly a bit more comfortable in our new home. We also made a 'chunder-chart' or 'vom-ometer', but that's down to your own discretion.

What if Freshers' Week isn't the best week ever?

I think the biggest myth regarding Freshers' Week is the assumption that it'll be the best week of your life EVER. For most, the reality is that this just isn't the case. Now, don't let this alarm you – for most people Freshers' Week is GREAT, but 'best week of your life'? Perhaps not.

Think about it ... Freshers' Week is your FIRST EVER week at university in an unknown environment with complete strangers. They'll inevitably become close friends (there's something about mutual experience that does that), but if you can naturally become *that* close with strangers in a week, think how much closer you'll be the week after, or the week after that, or in the second term, or in your final year – once you know each other inside out. *That* is when it'll start being the best time of your life, and each term will be better than the last.

Alternatively, if you don't find 'your people' straight away, don't panic. University will bring so many opportunities to meet new people, and you certainly won't be the only one not to click with your housemates instantly. You've got your course, your accommodation, your clubs, your societies and countless other chances to meet the people who get you.

What I'm saying is, embrace Freshers' Week and have the best time you can, but if it isn't quite what you anticipated, don't worry at all. Your 'best week ever' will come, and I'm sure it'll be at uni, but don't put too much pressure on seven days when you're at your most tense, vulnerable and dislocated. After all, anticipating it as if it's going to be pure euphoric bliss won't be helpful if things don't go to plan.

How do I avoid Freshers' Flu?

You can't. It literally isn't possible. From this point onwards, every lecture you attend will be drowned out by a symphony of coughs – a ca-cough-ony, if you will – from fellow freshers in the auditorium. The first time you get sick at uni won't be fun, but it'll hit you eventually, and it'll hit you like Anthony Joshua when it does. So don't be surprised when it catches up with you, just embrace it. Strength in numbers, right?

I'd recommend packing a survival kit with your parents' help before leaving for uni, so that you have a bag full of the essentials. Believe me, you won't realise how much you appreciate your family stash of medicine until it suddenly isn't just a cupboard door away.

Be kind to yourself and take some time to take a step back and chill. Get well soon!

Binge-drinking

I'd be lying if I said there wasn't a drinking culture at university, and that's a beast that needs to be tackled. What I want to tell you right here, right now, is that if you don't drink, that is more than okay. You don't have to justify yourself to anyone, regardless of how many questions you are asked. It's a personal choice, and you can prove anyone wrong very quickly by having just as much fun as them, minus the booze. If you're ever made to feel uncomfortable, make sure the person who made you feel that way knows that it's out of order – probably once they're sober and less likely to be an arsehole about it.

Be sensible and make sure someone always knows your plans for the evening. Know your limits, too, and be extra careful when walking home in a city you're still acquainting yourself with. Sometimes Students' Unions will have services that help people home from a night out if they need it (like night buses), but always make sure you know how to get back.

Also, don't get arrested in your first (or any) week at university, because that'd suck.

Settling in

Finding your *feet* at uni is – if you'll pardon the foot pun – the first *step* you'll encounter before becoming comfortable in your new home of three, four or more years. Not everyone takes to it like a duck to water, because you're not a duck, and water bills are expensive. And it's okay not to feel settled instantly – you'd be in the minority if you did. In this section, I want to share some tips for settling in and embracing the fantastic opportunity you've been given.

Firstly, your bedroom or dorm should be your safe space. A lot of people bring loads of photos and possessions from home, as they associate these with feeling comfortable and at ease, but there definitely needs to be balance. Personally I think it's a good idea to make sure your uni dorm has some new things in it, too, which are exclusively yours and a product of your independent, adult life. Decorate your new room so that it's cosy and comforting, but not in a way that just replicates your life at home and constantly reminds you of what you're missing (see 'How to make your room your own', page 63). Over time, this room will become a second home, somewhere you look forward to returning to.

One thing I'd like to draw particular attention to is photos. As aforementioned, the majority of people bring a selection of photographs of their friends and family back home, and memories they made there. That's great, and it's such a good (and cheap) way of decorating your room. However, I'd also advise you to continue growing this collection of photos while at uni. In a digital world, it's so easy to forget to print physical copies of photos, but I'd encourage you – especially during your first term – to go and print some new ones. This will make you realise, and appreciate, all of the friends and memories you've made in your new environment. Add to your collection of photos throughout your time at university. You're making memories all the time, so don't just romanticise the ones from your life back home – celebrate the new ones, too.

Chat to your family often. I find that it's great to have a big family group chat where everyone can just message every now and then and stay in contact. You don't always need to have a two-hour phone-call catch-up (although these are very much appreciated every now and then, too) to stay in touch – sometimes just a message to know someone is doing fine is enough. Also, don't be afraid to ask for help or advice. It's a great idea to get some parental advice when you do the laundry or pay a bill for the first time, because it'll make you more confident and give them the opportunity to talk to you and still feel like they're helping you.

Also, learn to cook your favourite recipes from home (see 'How to cook', page 135). Asking whoever makes that perfect casserole to share their recipe with you is another great excuse to catch up with the people you care about. You'll feel a sense of comfort and security in having that meal that reminds you of home, while also having the independence to cook it yourself.

The mid-point of the term is when I'd recommend having family come to visit, or going home for a weekend if you want to do that. Enough time will have passed for you to hopefully feel comfortable at uni, and it'll break down what is a very long term into two smaller chunks. Some universities have a reading week mid-term, so this could helpfully coincide. I'd be reluctant to recommend anyone going home too early in the term, even if you are feeling homesick, as it might actually do more harm than good. I know a few too many people who went home in week two for a 'visit' and never came back. If you can stick it out and it won't negatively impact your mental health, then try. You can do it!

How to make your room your own

You don't need to pay big bucks to give your room a little bit more personality. Here are some super-easy DIYs to help jazz up your dorm ...

Have it all mapped out

This is a spin on the classic 'student with £2.50 world map on the wall of their uni dorm' for the avid traveller or gap-yah student. It's for keeping track of the places you've visited on the map using pins, and is an idea I got in a Starbucks in Prague – because they'd DIYed it in the shop, not because the Pumpkin Spiced Latte went to my head. All you need for this DIY project is the aforementioned £2.50 map (price may vary ... obviously), some Blu Tack, a corkboard or noticeboard (the same size as your map) and some map pins. You can buy an inexpensive box of map pins in assorted colours online, as I assume this isn't something most people have just lying about. This DIY wall art is a cool way of logging your travels and could be a cracking conversation starter. If this sounds right up your street, take the following steps:

1. Stick the world map to the outer frame of the corkboard using Blu Tack or tape.

2. Pop a map pin into each of places you've travelled to, piercing the map and pushing through to the noticeboard behind it.
3. Attach the corkboard to the wall – command strips leave the least amount of damage and are very sturdy; mine have never failed me!
4. Keep adding pins every time you travel somewhere and build it up over time!

Money on the mind

Another one for those who love travelling – this DIY project costs as much as you're willing to invest in it, quite literally. Basically, it's creating a piece of wall art using leftover foreign currency. What you'll need is a selection of notes from countries you've visited (you know, the odd dollar or euro or forint or yuan left in your wallet that you keep accidentally giving to retail staff thinking it's UK currency) and a picture frame. Then follow the steps below:

1. Take the picture frame apart and remove the card inside that holds it together.
2. Line up your currency notes with a space in between each one and stick them to the piece of card. Using double-sided tape may be your best bet to keep it looking slick.
3. Insert the card back into the picture frame.

4. Attach the picture frame to the wall. If you don't have hooks, command strips will be strong enough to hold it up!

Fully booked

One for book lovers, this project incorporates your favourite book covers and is a great way to spark a conversation. You can buy postcards of vintage book covers or classic novels, but if you want to make this project even cheaper, just save photo files of your favourite book covers and print them off. The only other thing you'll need is a picture frame. If you print off the book covers at 6 x 4 inches, you can usually buy photo frames with six slots specifically for this size print. Next – you know the drill by now – take the following steps:

1. Print out your favourite book covers.
2. Take apart the photo frame.
3. Insert the book cover prints into the photo slots.
4. Put the photo frame back together and stick to the wall – if you don't have hooks, command strips are your new best friend.

Living in London

University is one thing, but university in London? That's a whole different kettle of fish. I asked my wonderful friend Derin Adetosoye for some insight into her life as a student in the Big Smoke.

Was the Freshers' Week experience different to what you anticipated?

Derin: Surprisingly, it did actually live up to expectations! Freshers' Week is the one thing I can actually say went how I anticipated, and every single night there were probably about 10 different events to choose from. What I really liked was the fact that most of the events were mixed with all of the other universities across London. It was a super-social week (or three ...) where I was able to meet new people, have fun and step out of my comfort zone. Living in my university's halls of residence was definitely a bonus, as it meant that I always had a group of people to go out with and was always in the loop with what was going on that night.

Is it super-expensive living in London? Did you have to sell any organs on the black market to afford it?

Derin: That's an understatement! Some nights – like the student nights in more casual clubs – were super-cheap, with drink deals as low as £1.50 (which is practically unheard of in London). But other nights, if you wanted to go somewhere a bit fancier for drinks or an event, it would definitely have an impact on the bank account. Let's just say I spent £17 once on a G&T ... don't ask. Rent is also expensive. At first, I didn't have anything to compare it to, but when a friend informed me that she was paying a fraction of the price outside of London, I was shocked.

50 Shades of Cray! Is it harder to meet friends and maintain social relationships in such a large city?

Derin: Without a doubt, yes. A lot of us are super-independent and are constantly busy working towards whatever it is we're trying to pursue, which means that it can often be very difficult to find enough time to maintain friendships and social relationships! Another huge factor that I think impacts this is the distance between where everyone lives. Rent prices in London can vary majorly and due to this everyone is kind of scattered across the city.

Have you ever regretted your decision to study in London?

Derin: I'd be lying if I said I didn't have a couple of moments (particularly during my first year) when I was seeing how different an experience my friends were having at their campus universities and that sense of community, and I started wondering why my experience wasn't the same. But eventually I realised that the London university life really is incomparable! While I was getting upset about not having a fancy-dress party on campus, for example, I was being presented with opportunities that would only be possible if I was exactly where I was (like in fashion and finance), right here in London. So now that I'm in my third year I can definitely say that I have no regrets, as the experiences, opportunities and exposure I've gained from being in a city as incredible as London is something I honestly wouldn't trade.

CHAPTER 3

WORK

Time for a university reality check: you're actually here to get a degree. I'm sorry to thrust bad news upon you like this, but it's time to make like Rihanna (featuring Drake) and work, work, work, work, work, work.

Before I started at uni, bright-eyed and bushy-tailed, I had no clue what the difference was between lectures, seminars and tutorials, or how working so independently could possibly be stressful. Well, now that I'm a third year with eye bags so big Tesco would charge you five pence for them, I'm definitely well acquainted with the academic workload that life as an undergraduate brings. Don't worry, though – it's nothing a Red Bull (or the Tesco basics knock-off version of Red Bull) can't solve.

Contact hours

What are lectures?

Lectures are educational talks given by (usually) one person in front of a crowd of students. This person will be an academic in the field of study that you are learning about and will present some ideas or a discussion on the topic for roughly an hour. You will sit there frantically trying to handwrite or type EVERY valuable piece of wisdom that comes out of their mouth, and desperately hoping you're spelling everything correctly. Lectures will probably baffle you, and that's not necessarily a bad thing – if you knew everything already, you'd be the one at the front with the fancy jargon and the microphone. And you'd probably have the degree already. Remember that you are there to learn, regardless of how much everyone on your course already seems to know.

How to get the most out of lectures

1. Turn up. Seriously. I know at the start you won't even be able to contemplate the idea of missing a lecture – especially once you realise that some of us pay approximately £75 per contact hour in our degrees. However, I can assure you that once you're two weeks in with a perpetual hangover, you'll probably snooze that 9 a.m. alarm. Even though lectures are often

recorded and available afterwards, they are so much more beneficial when you're actually in the room.

2. Check your academic emails beforehand, as often keen-bean lecturers will send over some things to read in advance of the lecture. They're not just doing it because they live, laugh and love the subject; it's to help you. That said, prep work isn't *really* crucial to your understanding of the lecture, so there's no need to panic or skip the lecture entirely just because you haven't done any reading in advance. Most lecturers don't ask questions or require audience participation (aaaand breathe – you're off the hook), and you'll soon suss out the anomalies to this general rule of thumb.

3. Find the handout (if there is one) as soon as you enter the lecture theatre. You don't want to be the one darting your eyes around the room frantically when the lecturer tells everyone to turn to page 3 ...

4. Make sure you have everything you need in your bag. I'd recommend always having a laptop or notebook (in fact, always have a notepad handy anyway just in case your laptop inexplicably crashes or runs out of battery), pens, some highlighters, a water bottle, tissues and an emergency snack (you don't want your stomach rumbling so loud that the microphones pick it up).

5. If the lecture slides are available in advance, get them up on your laptop screen so you can just copy and paste any quotes into your notes as you go, as you'll rarely have time to type or handwrite the entire thing. If you don't have slides available online and the lecturer is flicking through them as if their pension depends on it, prioritise jotting down the name of the writer and the source (e.g. the book title). If it's a key idea and a definition, at least make sure you've got down the name of the idea/thing/theory. This way, you can always look it up later to fill in the blanks.

6. I always handwrite my notes using a black pen, a coloured pen (for names, key ideas and sources), a highlighter (for titles and sub-headings) and a notepad. Oxford Campus notepads are particularly good as they are set out so that they're easy to scan, in case you want a digital copy.

7. Ask questions at the end of the lecture by heading to the front and asking the lecturer face to face or by emailing them afterwards. They'll be more than happy (make that: completely and utterly elated) to discuss the topics in more detail.

What are tutorials?

Tutorials are academic contact hours in groups of roughly 3–10 people. These are discussion-based, with an academic tutor there to lead the conversation. They'll pose questions to the room, and there will probably be a few awkward silences. Or, depending on how well prepared the group is, a lot of awkward silences.

Tutors set your essays and the prep work. They *will* expect you to have done this work, so do it. I appreciate that this is easier said than done, but even a vague understanding of the work you've been set is better than not attempting it. You and the rest of the group will benefit so much more if you have all done the work you were set. Also, don't be afraid to speak up. Join a discussion – even disagree with other tutees. Everyone will benefit from your opinions and ideas, just as you will benefit from theirs.

What are seminars?

Seminars are like lecture-tutorial hybrids. They are groups of roughly 10–20 people, with a member of academic staff leading a discussion. There's also an element of teaching, however, and the professor will probably give mini lectures, followed by rounds of conversation and questions on the content. Again, prep work is pretty much vital, so definitely make sure you do invest time in reading everything you've been set in preparation.

One thing I'd like to add here is: don't worry if you find tutorials and seminars a bit overwhelming. Inevitably, at first, you'll probably feel like everyone seems to know so much about the subject that they should be given their diploma right now, and that might make contributing to class discussions a little intimidating. I vividly remember a module I did in my first year where I felt like the stupidest person in the room, and no matter how much reading I did, I always felt I was not one, but about six steps behind … and they were all on motorbikes. I reached out to my tutor via email to apologise for not contributing and to assure her that I was actually doing the prep work but couldn't quite grasp it. She sent back the loveliest email, reassuring me that the first year of your degree is just about mastering the act of pretending that you know what's going on. She attached links to some supplementary reading, which she thought would really help me, and when I read what she'd sent, it changed the game for me. It was the confidence boost I really, really needed, and I will never be able to express my gratitude to her enough. So the lesson is: if you are struggling, reach out to your tutor – they'll only want to help you, and they'll probably be able to empathise with the way you're feeling.

How to wake up for your 9 a.m. lecture

Time to – *Kylie Jenner voice* – rihiiise and shiiine. Here are some top tips to make sure you never miss a 9 a.m. lecture ever again.

- *Put your alarm on the other side of the room so you **have** to get out of bed in order to shut it up.*

- *Sleep with the curtains open so natural light comes through in the morning and wakes you up. (Note: This won't work for about 8 out of the 12 months in the UK because it won't be light in the mornings, but let's take what we can get ...)*

- *Plan to meet with a friend in the morning to walk to your lecture together. If a friend is relying on you, that'll force you to get out of bed so as not to let them down.*

- *Shift all of your clocks to the Dubai time zone. Your 9 a.m. start just became a 1 p.m. start. You're welcome.*

- *Circulate an email to everyone else on your course that the lecture is actually at 11 a.m., not 9 a.m. as they may have previously been informed. The professor can't lecture to an empty room, and so will have to adapt accordingly to when everyone else decides the lecture is.*

- *Put something in a slow-cooker before you go to bed that will be ready at 8.30 a.m., so you have to be awake to salvage it, or else the food burns along with your chances of passing your degree ...*

- *Storm the university. They can't stop all of us.*

- *Prep your bag the night before so you have less to do in the morning. Always have some biscuits or snack bars in the bag just in case you're running late and don't have time for breakfast.*

- *If you're more of a night owl or late worker, become nocturnal so your lecture is just before you go to bed, rather than when you've just woken up. To you, 9 a.m. is no longer early – it's late.*

- *Buy an alarm clock with a built-in water pistol that shoots you until you get out of bed. (Do these exist? If not, how do I patent this idea?)*

- *Remember that time is just a social construct and 9 a.m. is only perceived as early because that's what we've been told to think. We're being brainwashed.*

Alternatively ... try keeping a consistent sleep schedule so your body is used to waking up at a certain time. Try avoiding caffeine after 4 p.m., and going to bed slightly earlier so you wake up feeling refreshed. I don't know – I'm yet to crack it. To be honest, it's a miracle if I'm up and out of bed before midday.

Picking a dissertation topic

You've made it to your final year, and now you're set the biggest essay of your university career: the dissertation. *Small explosion, sirens wailing, children crying.*

Since you've got to spend so much time working on this one project, you need to make sure you're focusing on something you're actually interested in and excited to research. You've got to still love it at the end of the six months you spend working on it. Here are some tips for how to make the whole experience a tad less diss-tressing …

1. Spend at least a week actively researching all the different avenues you could go down, and be open-minded. Let yourself go off on weird tangents, because that's how you'll find something that genuinely fascinates you.

2. Build on what you've studied before. Don't be afraid to draw upon modules you have found particularly interesting during your degree, or ideas/concepts you have come across. You won't be able to reproduce work you've written about it in an exam before (this is called self-plagiarism), but your supervisor will be able to advise you on that.

3. Merge your interests. This is the perfect opportunity to bring your other interests and passions into your university work, so think about how you can find a fruitful cross-section between them and your subject. Definitely don't force it, because it should be a natural connection, but do take some time to ponder how you can link two things you love.

4. Pick a topic that you're excited to research. The only way this project is going to be fulfilling is if you look forward to working on it. Your life will be so much easier if you actively *want* to find out more about the subject area.

5. Don't try to be too unique. For an undergraduate dissertation, you don't need to produce totally ground-breaking research that is going to change the face of academia forever. Pick a thought-provoking topic that has been discussed by academics before in some capacity. A really key component of the dissertation is engaging with academic discussions, and then delivering your own response. Don't try to invent a new colour or disprove gravity.

6. Ask your dissertation supervisor questions. They want to help, and have been assigned to assist you with your project because they are interested in your subject focus. Email them *any* questions you have and they'll be delighted to help you out, no matter how silly they may seem to you.

Researching for the diss

Keep track of absolutely everything you research – it'll make your life so much easier in the long run. I kept a whole folder specifically for dissertation research, and filed everything from notes on scrap pieces of paper to in-depth analyses of books I'd read. One thing I absolutely swear by is a research log, where I keep track of page numbers, publishing info, ideas and quotes. An example of how to make one can be found on page 85.

Also, back up everything. Make sure you have a second copy of any work you do, because you don't want to be *that* person who loses their work (and their mind) when it all goes wrong.

When looking for information, utilise the bibliographies at the end of any work you read. This will point you in new directions and can be so useful. Also, if your university library doesn't have the books you need for your research, request them. If your uni can't purchase them, see if other local universities have them, or spend a day at the British Library, which has access to every book you can imagine. Most of these books take 48 hours to arrive at the British Library, but you can request them online if you have a Readers' Pass (free to get a-hold of – you just apply online).

Reading smart and how to research

Working hard is about the hours you're willing to put in, but working smart is a skill that can be learned to minimise the number of hours you actually need to dedicate to getting the work done. And the best thing is that, contrary to popular belief, it's actually something you can get better at.

First, identify what the primary, fundamental reading for your degree is – what are the core things you need to learn for your course? Also, just because I'm using the word *reading* here, this doesn't just apply to Bachelor of Arts degrees, which are more focused on the humanities. Science degrees (BSc) also require research and reading academic texts. It's always important to know exactly what the course is demanding of you, and what you'll be expected to know as a prerequisite for taking the exam.

Often, exams will offer you a choice of questions, or a choice of subjects to cover. Always research and revise slightly more than is being asked of you, as only having the bare minimum number of topics covered won't give you much room to manoeuvre during the exam, but at the same time, make sure you're focusing on quality rather than quantity (for more advice on how to revise like a pro, see '10 tips to ace your A Levels', page 22). In academia, the more detail and nuance, the better, so go deeper on key topics and know them like the back of your hand – as if you were looking at it through a microscope.

When researching, utilise your university's resources: they'll have a rich tapestry of literature covering any topic imaginable, and if they don't have what you want, they can usually order in books and journals. Websites like JSTOR are fantastic, too, but remember that these are online archives of journals, magazines and other publications, meaning they probably won't have anything from the past five years, when vital scholarly developments and discoveries may have been made. When it comes to researching your dissertation or more niche subject areas, the British Library is a free resource that can order any book to their Reading Rooms in London (near St Pancras Station). It's really worth spending a day there to use their resources, rather than forking out for a book you didn't really want to read in the first place. Just remember to register beforehand and bring ID with you on your first visit.

If you read an article, always remember to read the bibliography, too. Even if that particular article wasn't specific to your area of research, the bibliography may be the key to unlocking that *perfect* article. This is the section at the end of the piece that details the research the author did for their work – essentially their reading list. Bibliographies will help you find articles that may not appear in your other searches.

Also, talk to your professors. Academic staff are academic staff for a reason – because they've been there, done that and got the diploma. If there's something obscure that you're looking for, they'll often know exactly where to find it, or at least be able to point you in the right direction. They're ambulatory encyclopaedias, honestly.

Always start by reading the abstract and introduction to get an idea of what the article is going to discuss. Remember that academic articles aren't like fictional stories with a surprise ending or a sudden plot twist – they should describe their exact argument straight away. The conclusion is the next place you should go if you're in a bit of a rush or don't fancy reading the whole thing; it'll give you a bit more information and summarise most of what is said in the rest of the article.

If you're looking at a whole book that has various chapters, usually the introduction gives a brief outline of each one. Also make sure you read the contents page to see which chapters are of most use, as – spoiler alert – some won't be. Also, check the index at the back to find specific pages that mention key thinkers, places, historical events or ideas. Then head straight to those pages to save yourself time. Many academic texts have so much waffle that they could be covered in maple syrup, so don't expect to read all of them cover to cover. It's not necessary.

If you're looking at something online, use your computer's search option to find specific key words within the text. This will take you straight to the golden nuggets of information and, once again, save you time.

Bibliographies and research logs

Making research logs while preparing to write essays changed the game for me. It made utilising and referencing my research so much more straightforward and improved my level of organisation tenfold. It makes you feel so much more on top of the essay, even when you're 2,000 words under it. Here's an example of how to make one:

Author	Quote/Idea	Page	Publishing Info	Notes

Filling in the page numbers and publishing info of your sources will save you so much time when it comes to making a bibliography. Publishing info can be found on the first few pages of a book or article, or at the top of a webpage. Plus, adding a section for 'extra notes' leaves space to type up some quick analysis while you're entirely focused on it, so it triggers a memory later down the line.

The steps I would take are as follows:

1. Create the research log and fill in initial research.

2. Read back through all your research notes and identify core ideas and themes: come up with what your

argument will be, based on the research (try not to be too set on an argument before you do the research, otherwise you'll have confirmation bias*).

3. Colour code the research you've done based on the different themes or ideas – each colour will become a paragraph in your essay.

4. Fill in the gaps in your research now you know what your argument (or main focal point) will be.

5. Create an essay plan, using the colour coding you have previously done as a guide to how to break down the paragraphs. Move them around to find the best structure, so that it flows as well as possible.

6. Copy and paste the colour-coded quotes or ideas from your research log into the essay plan, so you know which ones you are going to utilise. This puts all the quotes that are the same colour under the same paragraph heading, making them easy to see as you go through.

* Confirmation bias is when you already have an idea in your head, and so your brain tailors everything you read to simply confirm the argument you've already come up with. This can lead to obstinacy, and too rigid a mindset that is unwilling to accept alternative ideas. You should do your initial research before deciding your line of argument, so you are properly informed on both sides of a debate.

7. Start writing the essay (but don't be afraid to stop and do some more research if it will benefit you – sometimes you only spot holes in your research when you come to write it all out in proper prose).

8. Refer back to the research log (with all the referencing info) to cite your sources for footnotes and endnotes.

9. Type up your bibliography, citing all the sources you've used, and everything else you read in preparation for the essay.*

10. Submit the essay, get a fantastic grade and celebrate.

Remember that just because someone has had their work published, that doesn't mean it's the gospel truth. Academia is a continuing dialogue, so feel free to disagree with the work you're citing – so long as you can back up why you disagree.

---

* Even sources you read but *didn't* reference in the actual essay will have influenced the way you think in some way. Therefore, it's important to include them in your bibliography. Plus, it shows you did even more research, so it's a win-win.

Understanding the university grading system

The university grading system is a funny one, because it makes absolutely zero sense to anyone who hasn't had it explained to them. When I started in my first year I had to actually google what the different number classifications meant, because I'd heard people discussing getting a 2:1 and didn't know whether to congratulate them or provide a shoulder to cry on. Because what on earth does '2:1' even mean? And who the hell thought that was what it should be called?

Basically, this is how the actual grades work, with a first being the highest achievement and a fail obviously not being ideal. (Quick disclaimer: Every university, and every department within every uni, is different; not all of them will assess you in the same way, and some may give different weightings to each year of the degree. Make sure you check your department website for the most accurate info. This is only a general guide.)

- First-class Honours (1st) = 70–100 per cent
- Second-class Honours
  1. Upper division (2:1) = 60–69 per cent. This is what most people aim for! I know you're probably used to seeing 90–100 per cent as the top marks at school, but that really isn't the case at university, especially for

humanities degrees where that literally isn't possible. If you were getting 100 per cent on your work, that work is publishable, which is highly unlikely in your first year (or at undergrad level). At uni, getting 65 per cent or above is jumping-around-the-room levels of exciting.

2. Lower division (2:2) = 50–59 per cent
- Third-class Honours (3rd) = 40–49 per cent
- Fail = 39 per cent or lower

Your grade will probably be based on a weighted average. So, each year you will need a certain number of credits to pass the year, which usually works out as six equally weighted modules (i.e. each is worth 20 credits, making 120 overall). In each module, you'll get a percentage mark, and an average mark will be calculated to make your overall grade. If you get above 40 per cent in each module, you can proceed to the next year of the course. If you don't, you'll have to retake the module before you can proceed.

Your first year, generally speaking, won't count towards your overall degree classification, but you will still need to pass the year. It's what's called a 'formative year', meaning you still take exams and do coursework as you do in the years which do count, and still get a grade at the end, but it won't impact your overall degree. You just have to get above 40 per cent to proceed to year two of the course, which *will* count. It's called a formative year because it sets everyone up to be at the same level, with many second- and third-year modules relying on everyone having the same level of knowledge as a prerequisite. It also teaches you how to study, research and write at undergraduate level. (Note: This is for *most* but not *all* universities.)

For most traditional three-year degrees, your grade in second year counts for 40 per cent of your overall degree qualification. Then your third-year grade will count towards 60 per cent of your overall degree qualification. This means that your grades in the third year are more heavily weighted, and so contribute more to your overall result.

A dissertation in your final year is worth the same number of credits as two modules. This means that instead of doing six modules per year like usual, you'll do four modules *and* the dissertation.

For modern languages, an extra year is slotted in between the second and third year, which is spent abroad in the countries your languages are spoken. For example, if you study French and Russian, you might spend the first half of the year in Paris and the second half in Moscow. You have to write essays during this year in order to have 'Modern Foreign Languages **with a Year Abroad**' on your diploma, but they don't contribute to your final grade.

There's also an option for non-languages students to take a year abroad during their degrees and study at partner universities around the globe. Again, the grade you get at the international uni won't impact your final degree classification. So if you studied for a year in Prague, you could put on your CV that you have a 2:1 in your Maths degree from Bournemouth University, and studied at Prague University for a year and got a 2:1 for that year. The year abroad isn't a degree, it's just an opportunity to experience a new culture and continue to learn while there. This varies from uni to uni, so check the 'study abroad' options on your institution's website.

Business and marketing students, as well as many science students – particularly physicists and chemists – will spend a year working in their industry as part of their degree. This means your degree will be four years long, but for one of those years you will be on a placement somewhere, gaining real work experience.

Then there's the case of an integrated Master's degree,* which is four years long. The weighting of each year varies depending on the course and university, so check your department's website, where they will have a full breakdown. Hopefully it won't make you have a full breakdown, too, though.

Feeling exhausted yet? Me too. I feel like I've spent so long typing all of that out that I deserve a degree in explaining degrees.

---

* A Master's is a further qualification, after you graduate from university. However, some courses (especially science-based subjects) will allow you to apply for an integrated Master's programme, which squishes the under-graduate and Master's degrees together.

What is an Honours degree?

A normal degree would just mean getting a pass or a fail at the end, but the 'Honours' part basically just means that you'll also have a grade classification attached to it. As in, you will not only have the degree, but it'll also be specified how well you did – so whether you got a 3rd, a 2:2, a 2:1, or a 1st. Most degrees will now be considered an Honours degree, because they will have this specific grade.

Alternative uses for your degree

Okay, so maybe you're wondering what those tuition fees are really paying for. A degree is just a framed piece of paper, right? WRONG. Here are 22 alternative uses for your degree, once you've secured it ...

In the frame:

1. A tray to carry your dinner on
2. A really big table-tennis racket
3. Put it over your bath and use it as a table
4. Something to lean on while writing
5. Attach a strap and wear it as a stylish cross-body bag
6. Display with the diploma facing the wall – very edgy wall art
7. An umbrella on a rainy day
8. A shield
9. Attach strings and turn it into a hat
10. A pillow ... for someone you hate

Out of the frame:

1. A table mat
2. Cut it up and write Christmas cracker jokes on it
3. A tissue for your tears
4. Turn it into an origami swan
5. Confetti
6. Scrap paper
7. Use it for papier mâché crafts
8. Sew it onto a T-shirt
9. Put it on your lap and use it as a napkin
10. A bookmark
11. A mat to wipe your feet on
12. A very tiny blanket

CHAPTER 4

BASIC SURVIVAL

Picture this: you're four weeks into your first term at university. You still haven't cooked anything more radical than chicken pasta. Your bedroom has become a cactus and succulent cemetery. You've accumulated enough dirty bowls and glasses in your bedroom to open a restaurant. You're down to your last fresh pair of pants, and you've already been putting off this moment by turning all of your others inside out. Yep, we've all been there.

Forget *I'm a Celeb* – I'm a broke, tired university student … get me out of here!

Fear not, however, as I've dedicated an entire section of this book to basic survival tips. From paying your rent to recycling, I've got you covered … Kirstie Allsopp and Greta Thunberg bundled into one. It's time to iron out the creases of your university experience.

How to find a student house

Finding a student house to live in once you move out of halls of residence is one of those crazy 'adult' things that life just never really prepares you for. You've just got to a brand-new city with a brand-new group of people and suddenly you have to choose where you want to live in that brand-new city and which brand-new people you want to live with for a whole year – WHAT?! However, I can't stress enough the importance of taking time before you sign to find something that is exactly right for you.

Finding housemates

First, let's talk about housemates. One of the cardinal rules for uni accommodation is: do **not** live with someone who you are romantically involved with. I'm sorry to have to say it, but no matter how utterly and deeply in love with them you are, not all relationships last and not all relationships end in an amicable way – so don't be that horror story of the person sharing a double bed with their ex for a year.

Okay, now we've got that out of the way, who *should* you live with? Consider how many people you want to live with. Do you want to live in a big house with lots of people, which is always busy, energetic and loud, or would you prefer to live in a smaller, quieter house with fewer people? It's very common for groups of friends to want to live together in an eight- (or more) bedroom house, but these often don't have massive social areas, unless you're willing to sell one of your kidneys in order to afford it. My friends and I had this exact issue – none of the houses with lots of bedrooms had sufficient kitchen or living spaces, so we decided to split in half and go for two houses that were close together. This meant two houses with social spaces, the opportunity to have dinner parties and host each other, and a bit of distance, which often only makes the heart grow fonder. Just because you don't live together, it doesn't mean you won't see each other. Plus, you've still got both your kidneys, which can only be a positive thing.

Also, do you want to live in a house of all girls, all boys, or a mix of the two? Think selfishly for a second and decide which would suit **you** best, and what will be the best environment for you to thrive in. The dream is that your housemates all get on like a house on fire … without actually setting the house on fire. Although that's quite likely to happen, too.

You want people who are reliable, friendly and trustworthy, especially when it comes to paying rent and bills. Living together is supposed to be fun, so don't pick two people to live with who you know will clash or be at each other's throats all the time. Volatile people are difficult to live with, and you need a good support system around you, especially once exam season comes around.

If you're planning to live with people you've never lived with before (as in, you didn't live with them in halls of residence), then it's worth meeting up to discuss your priorities. For example, what time do they wake up? What time do they go to bed? Are they wanting to host other people at the house a lot? How much are they willing to pay for rent, etc.? People often have very different budgets, so it's good to know you're all on the same page. Don't let anyone make you feel guilty for wanting to save a bit of money – there will be other people who also want to cut costs who you can live with. Alternatively, a lot of student houses have bedrooms which are all different sizes. If there's one double bedroom and three singles, and the double bedroom is considerably nicer, maybe think about having the person who wants that bigger room pay slightly more. Taking a smaller bedroom may mean you can pay less, which may be a good way of saving money if you don't intend to spend too much time in your room. Make sure you have this agreement written down and signed on a physical piece of paper, just in case. This is all important to discuss before signing your life (and student loan) away, as you don't want to end up being charged a fee you're not comfortable with.

Finding a house

In terms of finding a house, check out local estate agents or student rental websites. You can either browse the houses online or flick through catalogues in an actual estate agent's shop with some assistance (probably a bit more efficient). Usually if you tell an estate agent exactly what you're looking for, they can save you some time by just telling you which houses fit those specifications. Another option is to walk around the areas where you know there are lots of student houses, see which locations and streets you like and then look up houses on those streets online. Finally, speak to friends in the years above you who may be able to give some good advice or know of a really nice six-bedroom house they went to once. Also, some landlords only rent privately based on recommendations from current tenants, so it's worth asking around.

When it comes to viewing properties to rent, it's best to organise a scheduled appointment with an estate agent who will give you a tour. Knocking on the door and asking the students for a tour is fine, but there's a high chance they won't be home or will be too busy. Estate agents have to let tenants know at least 24 hours in advance that they're conducting tours, so they have a chance to tidy up, which means you've got more chance of being able to see every room in the house. Take pictures if appropriate so you remember what it looks like, but always ask the student before photographing their bedroom – because it's kind of weird if you just start snapping away.

Ask the students who live in the property for their honest opinions on the house, the location and, most importantly, the landlord. They will know the house better than anyone, and will be totally honest with you, as they have no vested interest in it being sold to you. Both a landlord and an estate agent have a financial motive for convincing you to rent that property, but the students will tell you if there's a mould problem or the house is falling apart or that not having a tumble-dryer is a struggle. Your best bet would be to have an organised tour with an estate agent initially and then, if you're serious about signing, pop round one time to ask the current tenants some questions and potentially have a second look around. They'll (probably) happily oblige. If anything, they'll be grateful that the house is being signed and this is the last time they'll be bothered by potential future tenants and annoyingly chirpy estate agents.

Make sure you're happy with all of the bedrooms and remember that – unless someone pays more for a specific room – you could end up with any of them. Often people draw straws or pick at random, so don't just remember the house for the nicest room there.

Some things to look out for:

- How many bathrooms are there? How many showers? How many toilets?
- How much storage space is there in the bedrooms? Is there under-bed storage?
- Do the rooms have double or single beds? Do all have the same?
- How much storage space is there for food – in cupboards and in the fridge/freezer?
- What are the desks and working spaces like? Are they big enough?
- How big is the living area? How big is the kitchen?
- How many chairs and sofas do they have? How many people can be sitting all at once?

- Is there a table to eat at? If so, how many chairs are there?
- What is the lighting like? Is there enough natural light?
- Is the landlord good? Do they respond quickly to issues that arise?
- How much do bills cost, and are they included in the monthly rent?
- How much noise is there on the street outside?
- What is the walking distance to your lectures, the library, the town centre, the supermarket, the doctor's surgery, the bus station, the gym and the sports centre?
- Are there places to dry your clothes after they've been washed?
- Is it a good space to host other people for dinner, house parties, etc.?
- Are there plug sockets where you would want them to be?

Is 'bills included' always a good thing?

One of the most valuable lessons I learned when looking for a house to rent is that landlords only ever rent out houses to make money. This means that 'bills included' – although sounding like a deal even Noel Edmonds couldn't negotiate* – is usually not actually that cost-effective. Most landlords will charge an extra tenner per person per week on top of rent fees

---

* Noel Edmonds used to host a TV show called *Deal or No Deal* – or, as I like to call it, Brexit before Brexit was a thing.

for you to have 'bills included', but that probably isn't how much the bills will cost. I can absolutely guarantee they'll be making a profit somewhere along the line.

Paying your own bills means the amount you pay is much more reflective of the energy you use, especially now that smart meters are being introduced. Also, if your energy supplier realises you're paying too much, it'll give you a refund or some credit. A landlord, on the contrary, will pop that straight into their purse and be able to buy themselves a nice Greggs sausage roll* with their extra income. Twelve times a day.

If you do get a chance to chat to the previous tenants of the house, definitely ask them how much they pay per week for the household bills and what energy provider(s) they're with.

* Vegan Greggs sausage roll also optional. Other sausage rolls are available.

How to avoid murdering your housemates

1. **Make a chore chart:** It may sound absurd, but treat those fuckers like actual children. Chores won't be magically done, and there will always be horrible tasks like cleaning the loo that no one will nominate themselves for. The best way to make sure you're living in an enjoyable (and not infectious) environment is to make a chore chart and take it in turns. Usually this just makes the tasks seem less daunting or time-consuming, as you'll soon realise that each person only has to take out the bins two or three times a term, max. Tick things off, stick gold stars to it – it doesn't matter; just make sure they're done, even if that means treating housemates who are all in their twenties like seven-year-olds.

2. **Washing up:** The pile of washing naturally builds up and up and up, until you find yourself playing a game of utensil Jenga every time you want to cook up a pasta bake. My four housemates and I made a cross out of masking tape on the kitchen worktop to divide it up into individual washing-up piles. This made it clear if someone hadn't been bothering to do their dishes and encouraged us all to keep on top of things. It's almost

too easy for there to be a few forks or bowls leftover and think 'not my problem', but having clearly defined personalised zones makes it inescapable.

3. **Compliment them:** Okay, I know this sounds weird, but hear me out. It's very easy to find yourself occasionally calling out messiness or that one coat that has been hanging on the back of a chair for six weeks now. House group chats are littered with passive-aggressive messages like *'Please just PLEASE could someone FINALLY remove that laundry from the washing machine lol as I've wanted to do mine for DAYS and am on my VERY LAST pair of underwear haha – seriously it's so annoying guys we need to stop doing this!! Xx'* over the course of the year, and this can cause some hostility. Everyone needs to complain sometimes, and that's totally valid, but you'll be respected more widely if you balance this with positivity. For example, if someone takes out the recycling, just say thanks. They'll feel appreciated for doing the task (and therefore be more likely to do it again), and there'll be far less animosity or tension next time you have to ask them to cut out their annoying habits. It's all about balancing complaints with compliments, so you're not just ranting and raving all the time.

4. **Make sure rent and bills are always paid:** Money is such a tricky one, and having to ask a friend to transfer a considerable amount of cash can feel extremely uncomfortable. One way to avoid this is just to send a message to everyone at the end of the month checking that everyone's paid what they owe in a very matter-of-fact way, and then using this opportunity to broach it if someone hasn't coughed up. Everyone should be understanding and take this seriously, so set the precedent that you always check in just before rent and bills are due to make sure everyone's paid. You can pass this off as a way of double-checking each time to make sure the payment is correct, rather than starting off by accusing people. Just be open and honest about it so no one gets ripped off.

5. **Splitting payments:** Leading on from the last point, there are lots of great ways to split payments that the house needs to make. Examples of this could be the more obviously shared payments like gas and electricity bills, as well as more minor transactions like purchasing toilet paper for the house. A great app for this is Splitwise, where you can upload your shared payments and then each person is charged their individual cut. This'll just save the awkwardness of everyone silently refusing to buy more toilet paper because *they bought it last time and the time before that*. The fact is, you're going to be in a really sticky

situation without essentials like loo roll, both metaphorically and physically. And that's gross.

6. **Don't get complacent:** Just because you live together now doesn't mean you should stop making an effort. It's almost too easy when you live with your mates to forget to actually make time for them and just hang out. What you could do is have a group meal one night a week, and either cook together or take it in turns. It's like a university version of *Come Dine With Me*, only probably best not to score each other in the back of a taxi afterwards. Mostly because taxis are expensive, and you live in the same house anyway so shouldn't be going that far.

The en-suite life

Okay, it's about time we spoke about bathrooms. I'm sure you're on the edge of your (toilet) seat. For me, having an en-suite was a bit of a prerequisite for halls of residence in first year – not because I'd ever had one of my own before, but because the prospect of sharing a bathroom with complete strangers was daunting, and a tad gross.

So it came as a bit of an unwelcome surprise to find out, upon arriving at my new casa, that I was sharing two bathrooms with 10 other people, and not living the En-Suite Life of Zack & Cody after all.

However, just like a Nicki Minaj music video, I'm sure you knew there was a *but* coming pretty soon. It was actually COMPLETELY fine. It was not a problem in the slightest and, after a very short time, it was just the norm. I rarely had to wait for the bathroom, if at all, and didn't find it invasive or uncomfortable in the slightest, and I'm sure (or, at least, I hope) I speak for all of my housemates when I say that.* So, I thought I'd clear up some things right here, right now.

* Of course, if you do need an en-suite bathroom due to a medical condition or other circumstances, then make sure you get one. Don't be shy about being totally honest with your uni or accommodation providers because a) they'll definitely have heard worse than whatever freaky things your body does, and b) their whole job is literally to help you – make them earn that salary and keep them busy.

Sharing a bathroom

1. **You never have to wait.** I thought sharing a bathroom would result in queues for the shower to rival those at Thorpe Park, or constantly having a corridor full of people doing that little jig you do when you need a wee but can't access a toilet in the next five seconds. However, everyone is on *such* different schedules and timetables that it's rare to ever find yourself waiting. There's always a pretty even split between morning showerers and ~~weirdos~~ night showerers, as well as a mix each day of people who have 6 a.m. sporting commitments, 9 a.m. lectures, a 2 p.m. hangover-induced lie-in or the whole day off. Basically, it's rare that any two people will have similar timetables, let alone the whole corridor.

2. **Life after halls of residence.** Once you move out of halls, en-suite rooms are like rare Pokémon ... if those Pokémon were three times as expensive as all the other ones. They just don't really exist. So why get used to the luxury, only to have it stripped from you like when *La La Land* was told it had won Best Picture at the Oscars, only to find out it wasn't them at all? Essentially what I'm saying is that, since you probably won't have an en-suite in later years' accommodation, why be fussy about it now?

3. **Stranger danger.** One of the main concerns regarding a shared bathroom is other people. It's not me, it's you. And I understand that worry. But the reality of the situation is that university housemates become very close, very quickly, and don't feel like strangers by day two. Plus, if people do have bad habits, there's honestly nothing an anonymous, passive-aggressive Post-it Note can't fix.*

4. **Cleaning the bathroom.** A lot of halls of residences that have shared bathrooms will employ cleaners to keep them looking spick and span so that you don't have to. However, if this isn't the case, your best bet is to come together as a group and set up a cleaning rota. Realistically, if divided up on a weekly basis, you'll probably have to clean the bathroom for one week out of the whole term, which is pretty much nothing. Plus, if you had an en-suite you'd be cleaning it every week every term, so there's actually less cleaning required of you. Teamwork makes the dream work.

5. **Cleaning yourself.** The ultimate hack when sharing a bathroom is to have a wash bag or shower caddy that

* Passive-aggressive notes or group-chat messages are an integral part of your university living-with-other-young-people experience. However, I'd always recommend speaking to people face-to-face in as reasonable a way as possible – it's always hard to judge the tone of a message, so they can cause unnecessary tension.

is portable and can therefore be carried between your bedroom and the bathroom. This way, your products don't become public property like at a fancy spa (except it's uni accommodation and there is literally nothing fancy about it) and transporting your things couldn't be easier. Also, if you keep your toothbrush, hairbrush, etc., with you, then you know they're not being used by anyone else. Also, you could wear flip-flops or sliders in the shower if you're that concerned about other people's funkiness, but I can guarantee that after a fortnight you'll be so comfortable with the people around you that you won't even think about it.

How to do laundry

There's absolutely NO shame in asking your parents to walk you through it the first time you do your own laundry. They'll appreciate still being able to help you out. Plus, it'll give you confidence that you're doing it right and not about to end up with clothes that could dress a Sylvanian Family rather than a uni student. To help you along, here are the essentials:

1. Split clothes into lights (whites and light pastels) and darks (anything else): if you add a bright red top to a white wash, you will end up with the wardrobe of Peppa Pig. You can get washing baskets that have two separate compartments for lights and darks, and I'd really recommend getting one. You can also add an additional pile for colours (i.e. reds, greens, etc.) if you want to be more specific.

2. Check the labels on your clothes to see what the washing instructions are. Some clothes will say that they are not machine washable and need to be washed by hand, or can't be washed above a certain temperature. Unless you want a whole wardrobe of crop tops, this is vitally important. Do this for EVERY SINGLE GARMENT because they WILL be different. I cannot stress this enough. If it says 'Dry clean only', they didn't just put that there for fun.

3. Also check the labels for whether clothes are tumble-dryer safe – it might be a good idea to write down which clothes *aren't* safe to go in the washing machine or tumble dryer so that you know for next time.

4. Separate out clothes into different washes depending on how heavy the fabric is. For example, jeans, jumpers and towels can usually go at a higher temperature than lighter fabrics like T-shirts and delicates.

5. Put the detergent into the machine, then pop the clothes into the barrel. Make sure the barrel is no more than three-quarters full. You can also add some fabric softener if you want to keep your clothes extra nice – it's definitely worth it.

6. Choose your wash cycle and temperature based on the clothes you're putting into the wash. Whites will generally go at a higher temperature, and darks at a lower one. Press go!

7. If you don't have a dryer, make sure you'll be home when the clothes are finished in the washing machine. Hang them up straight away, as if they're left festering in their sogginess, they'll just start smelling damp, and then they'll stink more than *before* they went in. If you do have a dryer, remove the clothes that aren't tumble-dryer safe, then whack that baby on.

8. Hang wet laundry on a clothes horse (or clothes pig, or clothes sheepdog – depending on how big it is), then, once dry, fold it and put it away.

Fabric care symbol guide

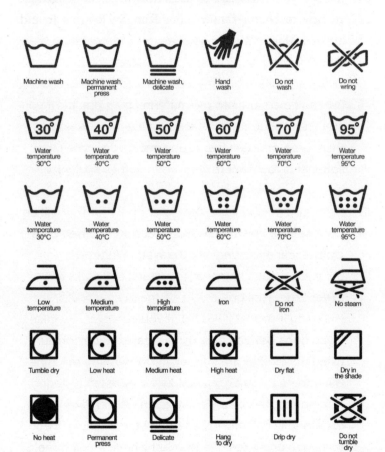

How to use an iron

Even though I can count on one hand the number of times I've used an iron at university (oh the iron-y), it's a crucial life skill and one you might as well learn now. So, look no further. This is how to channel your inner Robert Downey Jr and become Iron Man.

1. Set up an ironing board – these are designed to absorb heat and moisture without suffering any damage. If you don't have an ironing board, use a flat, sturdy surface like a table or countertop – just make sure it isn't flammable. Obviously.

2. Get your iron and fill up the water reservoir. This will be a compartment with a section that opens or detaches, and you can tip in water using a jug.

3. Lay out the wrinkly garment on the ironing board, arranging it so that it lies flat. If you iron over a wrinkle then you're just going to iron a creased line into your garment.

4. Turn on the iron. The metal section will begin to get hot – and fast. Suffice to say, don't touch it. See the 'Extra rules' on page 117 for exactly how hot to make the iron depending on the fabric.

5. Run the hot, flat side of the iron slowly and firmly over one side of the garment and smooth out those wrinkles like a middle-aged person on Photoshop.

6. Tackle each part of the garment separately. If it's a shirt, for instance, iron the collar, sleeves, cuffs and main body in turn.

7. Flip the piece of clothing over, smooth it out and repeat the process on the other side. In order to avoid making creases on the other side, you could put the item around the ironing board (as if you're dressing it) so that it isn't double-layered beneath the iron.

8. Hang up the item on a hanger and you're done! Now on to the next one ...

Extra rules:

- *For woollen garments, place a damp cloth between the item and the iron.*

- *For silk, turn the item inside out before ironing.*

- *Use a low setting on the iron for acetate, silk, wool and rayon, a medium setting for polyester and a high setting for cotton. The clothes label will tell you what the item is made from.*

- *If you're ironing different fabrics which need different settings, channel your inner Drake and start from the bottom. Use the lowest heat setting first, then work your way up so that you don't have to wait for the iron to cool down and heat up again each time.*

- *Using filtered water apparently helps avoid calcium build-up in the iron, but I'm not sure how many student houses have access to fancy-pants filtered water, so this is a pretty minor point. I like my water like I like my Instagram posts: #NoFilter.*

- *Don't rest the iron on the clothes, because they will burn. Obviously.*

How to recycle

You don't need to be Greta Thunberg to know that there are really easy things you can do every day to live more sustainably and look after the planet. Recycling is probably the easiest way to do this.

Recycling bins are usually taken out once a fortnight. You should check on your local council website to see which day it is, then write it down on a noticeboard or on a Post-it Note on the bin so that it's impossible to forget. Your local council website is also a good place to get information on what can and can't be recycled in your area.

Most houses will have a designated recycling bin, which can be filled with anything recyclable (which we'll get on to in a moment), but other councils require you to put your glass into a box, and everything else into a bag. These should be provided by the council, so if your student house doesn't have them (or they're stolen by drunken revellers), request that they're delivered to you free of charge.

So, what can be recycled?

- Newspapers, magazines and catalogues
- White paper, including shredded paper
- Envelopes (including ones that have windows)
- Brown paper
- Non-shiny wrapping paper

- Cardboard boxes (cereal boxes, dishwasher tablet boxes, Amazon delivery boxes)
- Milk bottles
- Plastic drinks bottles
- Shampoo and shower gel bottles
- Detergent and soap bottles (but remove the pumps)
- Bottles of bleach, or other cleaning products
- Plant food and pesticide bottles
- Skin-care product bottles
- Pots that contained yogurt, desserts or soup
- Tubs that contained butter or ice cream
- Trays/punnets that contained fruit, meat or ready-meals
- Trays for biscuits and chocolate boxes
- Brown plant pots
- Drinks cans
- Food tins (push the lids inside)
- Chocolate and biscuit tins
- Aluminium foil (with no food residue)
- Aluminium trays and tubes
- Glass bottles of any colour
- Jars (i.e. for sauces or jam)
- Non-food bottles and jars (perfume, aftershave, beauty creams, etc.)

Remember to ...

- Remove plastic wrapping that some magazines come in
- Empty and rinse bottles and replace any lids
- Leave labels on, as they'll be removed as part of the recycling process
- Squash bottles to save space
- Give your pots, tubs and trays a quick rinse so that food residue doesn't ruin other recycling
- Put metal lids and caps back on your glass containers

Did you know?

- If you scrunch paper and it doesn't spring back, that means it can be recycled.
- You should not recycle bottles that used to contain corrosive chemicals (like antifreeze) because they could harm the staff who work on the recycling process.
- You can't recycle paint pots at home, but you can take them to your local recycling centre, which can do it for you.
- Your local recycling centre can also recycle general kitchenware (like cutlery, pots and pans), as well as metal containers that once contained chemicals (like white spirit), light bulbs and any other metal items around the home (like kettles, irons and pipes).

Things that can't be recycled:

- Bubble-wrap
- Sweet packets or wrappers
- Laminated pouches (i.e. for cat food and coffee)
- Toothpaste tubes
- Medicine packets
- Expanded polystyrene
- Crisp packets
- Glass cookware like Pyrex
- Drinking glasses
- Vases
- Microwave plates
- Nail varnish bottles
- Sanitary products (including nappies)
- Any medical items such as needles, syringes or blood bags
- Pet litter
- Animal bedding

How to budget

No more livin' la vida broke-a!

Food

1. Keep your receipts for all food shops. If you have to chuck something out because it went off before you could eat it, make a note of that on the receipt so that you reconsider before buying it again next time.

2. Check the 'best-before' dates on food at the supermarket. Often, if you dig a little deeper or lift up the crate, you can find the same product with a later 'best-before' date. Obviously, if you're going to use the food soon, you don't need to do this. However, if you're not 100 per cent sure when you'll be using the ingredient then this can prevent waste.

3. The bigger the supermarket, the cheaper the products will be. It's true – convenient, smaller 'express' stores on big high streets charge slightly more for exactly the same products. Also, if the more budget stores are out of town, see if there's a bus that can take you there. Often you can get really cheap all-day bus tickets with a student card.

4. Meal plan, meal plan, MEAL PLAN. This ensures you're only buying the essentials, and nothing will go to waste.

5. Go to the greengrocers or market instead of buying fruit and veg from the supermarket. Usually the fruit is bigger, cheaper and more sustainably grown.

Banking

1. At the beginning of the year, most banks will have promotions for setting up a student bank account. Check out what each one has to offer and go with the deal that best suits you. Some banks will send you an Amazon gift card, while others will offer you a free student railcard.

2. Setting up a separate account with Revolut or Monzo is a good way of compartmentalising money. They have great mobile apps that keep track of where you're spending, what you're spending money on and whether you're on budget for the month. They're also really easy to transfer money to and from, and can be 'frozen' (rather than cancelled) at any time if you temporarily misplace your card and have **the panic**.

3. Always make sure you've factored in bills and rent money before budgeting for the month. That money *has* to be paid.

4. Be cautious with overdraft allowances. Remember that money has to be paid back at some point, and can be a horrible slippery slope.

Discounts

1. Students often get discounts in retail stores. You can get a National Union of Students (NUS) card, use UNiDAYS (free) or make a StudentBeans account.* Some stores will just need to see your campus card, though. Also, student discount promotions are usually doubled around the time when a new term begins and Student Finance England sends you some funds if you've secured a student loan (see 'How does student finance work?', page 187). Make the most of these opportunities to save!

2. In university cities, most independent restaurants and shops will use a student discount as a promotion to get new students to have a snoop around.

---

* These are initiatives you sign up for in order to be able to use your student discount. They often host special offers around the beginning of term, too.

3. Tourist attractions in university cities, and around the world, often have student discounts or free access for students. Always keep your student card in your wallet and make sure you ask, as you never know when it'll come in handy. Go get more culture than Cardi B's daughter.*

4. Pick up loyalty cards for your favourite coffee shops, hairdressers and retail stores. You could get yourself a little freebie every now and then.

5. Sign up for email alerts from your favourite restaurants and shops, who will let you know about any discounts or promotions they're running. Often apps are a really great way of finding these, too. This is especially handy around Christmas or your birthday, when you'll likely be sent some sort of discount.

6. It's really worth getting a railcard if you commute via train frequently. You'll have to pay for this, but the fee for my railcard was covered by the savings I made on my first journey.

* Cardi B's daughter is called Kulture. This was a poor attempt at trying to insert a pop-culture reference into a section about budgeting.

Freebies

1. Freshers' Fair is the ultimate freebie opportunity. It'll be like *Supermarket Sweep*, except it's 90 per cent MAOAMS. The only price you have to pay is signing up to a newsletter, and probably talking to an enthusiastic representative at the desk for two minutes. I'm still getting the Dog Walking Society emails three years on.

2. Student houses do not need to pay Council Tax.

3. Employers will often have promotional stalls or events with loads of (usually edible) freebies. I remember going to a computer-science pub quiz put on by a major accounting firm, despite neither studying computer science nor having any interest in accounting as a career. However, they had a free bar, and someone has to come last in the quiz to make everyone else feel better about themselves, right?

Other tips

1. Do a 'Secret Santa' with your university friends rather than buying gifts for everyone individually.

2. Some services, like Uber, Airbnb and Deliveroo, will give you free credit if you refer a friend and they buy through your link.

3. Regardless of how much your income is, set aside a weekly allowance, which is just the bare minimum of what you actually *need* to spend.

4. Sell your old textbooks to students in the year below you, and sell old clothes you no longer wear on websites like Depop.

5. Eat before going for a food shop. Never shop on an empty stomach.

6. One easy way to make some quick money is to participate in market research or dissertation research. People also make money at uni by photographing events or working at major events that need temporary staff.

How to pay rent

1. When signing a housing contract, every tenant will need a UK-based guarantor. This basically means someone who will bail you out if you fail to pay your rent. It's worth having this sorted before you start looking for accommodation, as often letting agents won't give you much time to sign the contract.

2. Each housemate will probably need to pay a deposit, which you'll get back at the end of your tenancy, providing everything is in order and no drunk idiots have punched a hole through the wall.

3. Make sure you all pay on time every month. Setting up a Direct Debit or standing order is a good way of doing this so the money leaves your account automatically.

Tip: Be nice to your landlord and show gratitude when they help sort out a problem in your house. We had such a good relationship with our 70-year-old landlord, which just made him more eager to replace things in the house that weren't working, and he checked on us regularly to make sure we were all good. One time, he even tried to facetime me, but I couldn't pick up as I was in a lecture. When I called him back, he just wanted to ask how my trip to Paris had been. I'll always regret missing that call.

How to pay bills

Bills, bills, bills. As much as we hate them, they've got to be paid. Here's how to do it …

1. If you can, chat to the previous tenants of your student house. They'll be able to give you a rough idea as to how much you should expect to pay per person per month, as well as let you know which energy/water/ broadband providers they were using.

2. Use comparison sites to find the best deal on service providers. Fees are usually worked out on an average per-month system – meaning that, despite using significantly less energy in the summer months due to not needing to heat the house, you pay the same amount every month. In the summer months you over-pay, and in the winter you under-pay, so that it all balances out.

3. Call up the service providers or set up a profile online. If you can get a smart meter installed in the house (free of charge) then do so – they're much more sustainable as they send constant updates to energy companies about how much energy the country needs, so there's much less wastage.

4. I'd really recommend setting up a separate account that everyone pays into, or an app such as Splitwise that automatically splits fees between all housemates fairly. It can be difficult having to chase your friends to pay bill money, so avoid it if you can!

5. Make sure you pay on time each month. Setting up a Direct Debit or standing order is a good way of doing this so the money just leaves your account automatically.

6. If you end up using less water/energy than you've paid for, then the provider will refund you or give you credit at the end of the year. If you've used more than predicted, you'll have to cough up that money.

Tip: Some landlords will have a 'bills included' option for paying rent. This saves some hassle, but it's important to remember that they're probably making a profit in some way from offering this. It's often much cheaper to sort out your own bills. (See 'Is "bills included" always a good thing?' on page 102 for more detailed information on this.)

How to read meters

The other day my housemate told me how electricity is measured, and I was like, Watt!? Here's how to read the various kinds of meters you might find in your student house.

Tip: Smart meters will send your readings straight to the service provider, making them as accurate as possible and saving you having to read the rest of this page. Installation is free *and* they help save the planet, so if you won't do it to save your own time, do it to save the planet David Attenborough loves.

Electrical meters

Dial electrical meters

Some older electricity meters will have dials instead of digits, which is the least helpful thing in the whole entire world. I'd definitely recommend writing them down as you go along, as it's so confusing and easy to lose track of. On the plus side, you'll feel like Alan Turing trying to crack a crucial code. Or a contestant on The Crystal Maze.

1. Read the numbers on the dials from left to right.
2. If the pointer is between two numbers, write down the lower one. However, if the pointer is between 0 and 9 then it's a 9.

3. If the pointer looks like it's exactly on a number but the reading on the dial after it is nine, that means it hasn't quite reached that number yet. So, go for the number below it. In the diagram below, the third dial is pointing very close to 7. However, since the dial after it (the fourth dial) is a 9, we'd read the third dial as 6 not 7.

So the meter reading below would be: 94694.

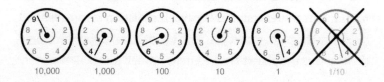

Digital electrical meters

1. Read your meter display from left to right.
2. Ignore any numbers that appear after a decimal point or space.
3. Ignore any numbers in red.

Gas meters

Imperial gas meters

1. Read the first **four** numbers from left to right, including any zeros at the beginning. You need to submit a four-digit number.

2. Don't include any numbers in red, or anything after a red number.

3. If your meter reaches 9,999, it'll reset back to zero.

Metric gas meters

1. Read the first **five** numbers from left to right, including any zeros at the beginning. You need to submit a five-digit number.

2. Don't include anything after a space or decimal point.

3. If your meter reaches 99,999, it'll reset back to zero.

How to keep houseplants alive

- Literally just water them.
- That's it.

How to cook

When I arrived at university, it's safe to say that my cooking ability was lacking somewhat … or entirely. Let's just say that the smoke alarm definitely worked, and I made sure to test it regularly, albeit unintentionally. If anything, I reckon it was a tad too sensitive. No one likes a drama queen, right? Then again, no one is ecstatic about a flaming omelette either.

However, cooking is something you can definitely get better at. It's definitely a case of trial and error. It's just that some of the errors could potentially poison your guts … but we all love a challenge.

Meal planning

Meal planning is the fine art of working out how you can most cost-effectively buy and use ingredients, so that you're not a) Usain Bolt-ing it to the supermarket every evening or b) chucking enough to feed a small tribe into the bin every fortnight once you finally accept that the green fuzz is there to stay.

Your best bet is to find different ways of using the same ingredients to make a completely different meal with only one or two items substituted or added, so you have some variation without wasting loads or spending a small fortune. For example, a pack of frozen chicken breasts could last for a week and be used to make chicken pasta, curry, chicken wrapped in bacon, and fajitas. The veg you buy to go alongside this can be utilised in multiple meals.

Alternatively, you could bulk-cook something in a big batch, like a bolognese or a chilli con carne, which will require you to buy fewer ingredients. You can just heat these up whenever you're in a rush and can't be bothered to cook, or when you fancy something a bit easier.

Quick cooking tips

So, it's the first week of having to fend for yourself, and suddenly your ineptitude in the kitchen has turned from a funny incompetency to a survival crisis. It's time to learn – and fast. Just remember that Gordon Ramsay didn't slip out of the womb with a spatula in hand (ouch for Mrs Ramsay ...) or his 16 Michelin stars awaiting his inelegant arrival on a silver platter. Everyone starts somewhere, and eventually you, too, could be kitchen-savvy enough to scream at someone that they're an idiot sandwich.

Like many of you, I had genuinely no clue how to use anything in the kitchen when I first crashed into university. For a while, everything I produced had a certain 'chargrilled' look to it (my less generous housemates might use the words 'incinerated' or 'cremated' instead) and recipe-book jargon confused the hell out of me. 'It means the number of degrees the oven needs to be turned to, idiot!' shouts my bemused housemate, prising a casserole dish and a protractor out of my oven mitts. Now it made sense why my lasagne had slipped out of its dish when propped at 160 degrees ...

So with this section, I wanted to share my top tips for student cookery, which I learned in my three years at uni. Just like a cake, it's time to *rise* to the occasion.

Rice, Rice, Baby: To cook rice, follow this simple rule: for every cup of rice you have (I find it useful to use a mug to measure this), you'll need one and a half cups of water. Start by tipping your dry rice into a sieve and washing it under a cold tap. Then put the washed rice in a saucepan, add your one and a half cups of water and bring it to the boil. Once the water has boiled, reduce to a low heat and put a lid on the pan until all the excess water is gone. This should make your rice lovely and fluffy.

Pasta: Why, when I try to cook pasta for one, do I cook so much that a small nation could survive on it for a week? This is a mystery I've been trying to solve for a while now, but I eventually realised that there's a way to work out how much you actually need. Pour the dry pasta from the packet into the bowl you'll be eating it from, and determine your perfect sized portion. Then just tip it straight from the bowl into your pan for cooking! This way there's no waste. When cooking pasta in boiling water, add salt to the water to make it salty like the sea ... or a friend you didn't text back. This will make your pasta taste infinitely better.

Keep it tasteful: Don't forget to *taste* what you're cooking as you go along, rather than realising once it's already on your plate that you made it too salty. Add your seasoning slowly and check how the food tastes regularly. This will also help you to understand herbs and spices (don't be afraid to experiment!), as you'll notice when a dish could be elevated, and know how to do so.

Metal can't go in the microwave: Seriously.

Keep it *Frozen* like Anna and Elsa: When cooking for one, it can be difficult to keep all your ingredients fresh. I'd really recommend buying frozen veg, which can just be defrosted whenever you need it for a dish, rather than turning your assigned shelf into a broccoli graveyard. Freezer bags (or ziplock bags) are great for this and can be washed out and reused. Keep an eye on use-by dates for meat as well, and freeze it if it looks like you won't have time to eat it before then.

The greengrocer's got you covered: I found that shopping for fruit and vegetables at a greengrocer's (rather than a big supermarket) was much cheaper and more sustainable. They use a *lot* less plastic and the individual fruit/veg you buy is usually bigger. You can also reduce waste by buying the exact quantity you need.

Oil me up: If you're cooking something in the oven and want to make it crispy like Walker's, oil is your new BFFL. Drizzle it on top of potato wedges and veg for that lovely crispy taste.

Basic essentials for your first shop

A couple of years ago a certain upmarket supermarket (whose target demographic definitely does not include broke students) released a list of 'store-cupboard essentials', which included Swiss vegetable bouillon powder and rose harissa paste. If you're as confused as I am and got lost after the word 'bouillon', don't worry, I've got you covered. These are the actual essentials that you'll find yourself using on a daily basis. Here's what to stock your cupboards with on day one … Just remember, you don't need to fill your cupboards as if the apocalypse is imminent.

- Salt
- Pepper
- Sauces (ketchup, mayo, BBQ, etc.)
- Garlic
- Mixed herbs
- Chilli powder
- Cooking oil
- Soy sauce
- Rice
- Pasta (penne, spaghetti, etc.)
- Noodles

- Onions
- Peppers
- Baked beans
- Stock cubes
- Gravy granules

Cheap and easy meal ideas

Pasta

- Spaghetti and meatballs
- Spaghetti bolognese (see page 144)
- Spaghetti carbonara
- Spaghetti with garlic prawns
- Tortellini/ravioli
- Penne pasta with chicken and bacon
- Pasta with pesto and chicken
- Pasta bake (tuna/pancetta/veg)
- Mac 'n' cheese
- Lasagne

Eggs

- Frittata (see page 156)
- Omelette (see page 155)
- Spanish tortilla

Noodles

- Stir-fry
- Pad Thai

- Noodles with soy sauce and edamame beans

Chicken
- Chicken wrapped in bacon (with cheese and pesto inside)
- Chicken nuggets (see page 145)
- Chicken in soy sauce (see page 151)
- Chicken stir-fry
- Chicken fajitas
- Chicken korma
- Chicken tikka masala
- Chicken pie
- Chicken hotpot
- Chicken with lemon/orange

Meaty Dishes
- Sausage and mash
- Sausage or beef casserole
- Quesadillas
- Tacos
- Sweet and sour pork
- Pork chops (with honey and mustard)
- Chilli con carne
- Thai green curry
- Pizza
- Burgers
- Toad in the hole
- Shepherd's/cottage pie

Fishy Dishes

- Salmon fillet with rice/noodles and veg
- Prawn cocktail
- Fishcakes
- Baked fish
- Paella

Veggie Ideas

- Baked aubergines
- Vegetable bake
- Nut roast
- Pizza
- Veggie burgers
- Halloumi and avocado fajitas
- Halloumi and roasted veg
- Pea and asparagus risotto
- Butternut squash risotto
- Tomato and onion tart
- Sweet potato and vegetable curry
- Falafel wrap

Breakfast Ideas

- Eggs (see page 154)
- Porridge
- Granola and yogurt
- Muesli
- Cereal
- Bacon/sausage (or both) sandwich

- Avocado on toast
- Jam/Nutella/peanut butter on toast
- Pancakes
- Pastries
- French toast
- Full English

Lunch Ideas

- Soup and bread
- Sandwiches or rolls
- Jacket potato
- Last night's leftovers
- Hummus and veg/breadsticks
- Croque monsieur
- Fish finger sandwich
- Panini
- Bruschetta
- Beans on toast

Recipes

These are some of the easiest recipes I know – and they are all delicious!

Spag Bol

Spag bol is an absolute classic, and a staple of university cooking, as it's pretty much the first thing everyone learns to cook. This is a simple recipe that can be made in 30–40 minutes with minimal prep – perfect for evenings when you don't really have much energy. It's also great to reheat for future meals.

What you need
250g spaghetti
1 × 500g pack beef mince
olive oil, for frying
1 onion, peeled and diced
1 garlic clove, peeled and chopped
1 × 400g tin chopped tomatoes
1 beef stock cube
salt and pepper, to taste

Method

1. Brown the mince in an oiled frying pan over a medium-high heat to get rid of any excess fat. Place the mince in a bowl and wipe down the pan with some kitchen paper.
2. Fry the onion in some oil (in the same pan) over a medium-high heat. Once it starts to go translucent, add in the garlic and fry for 2–3 minutes.
3. Add the mince back in and mix it all together.
4. Add the tinned tomatoes and half a glass of water, along with the beef stock cube. Reduce the heat to low-medium and let it simmer for 15–20 minutes or until it starts to thicken slightly. Have a taste and season as necessary with salt and pepper.
5. While you're waiting for the sauce to cook, put your spaghetti in a saucepan of salted boiling water for about 8 minutes
6. Drain the pasta in a colander and serve in a bowl topped with the sauce – and feel a sense of accomplishment. If you cook this in a big batch you've got an easy meal for another day!

Homemade Chicken Nuggets

My housemate Ella makes the most incredible homemade chicken nuggets, and she's kindly shared the secret formula with me for this book. This is so simple and – I'm going to say it – better than anything I've ever had from McDonald's.

What you need
250g cornflour
pinch of salt
pinch of black pepper
pinch of paprika
2 eggs
2 chicken breasts
4 tbsp vegetable oil

Method
1. Add the cornflour, salt, pepper and paprika to a shallow bowl and mix.
2. In another shallow bowl, beat the eggs until they're combined.
3. Chop the chicken breasts into bite-sized 'nuggets' (always wash your hands after handling raw chicken).
4. Coat each chicken piece in the cornflour mixture first, then dunk it in the egg mixture, then re-coat with the cornflour.
5. Heat the oil in a frying pan over a medium-high heat and fry the nuggets until golden brown and cooked through (this should take about 3 minutes per side).*

* Undercooked chicken can give you food poisoning, so make sure the nuggets are fully cooked through and piping hot before serving. If you're unsure, cut one in half to be certain.

Homemade Potato Wedges

I love this simple method from my head to my pota-toes.

What you need
4 large potatoes
drizzle of olive oil
pinch of salt
pinch of black pepper
pinch of paprika

Method
1. Preheat the oven to 180°C/350°F/Gas 4.
2. Peel your potatoes and chop them into wedges.
3. Coat them in the olive oil, salt, pepper and paprika in a shallow baking tray and bake for 25 minutes, stirring halfway through, until browned and crisp.

Shakshuka

This is a Middle Eastern-inspired dish, which I discovered on a trip to Tel Aviv. It's super-simple, so delicious and – most importantly – CHEAP! This is just as delicious for dinner as it is for brunch.

What you need

2 red peppers, chopped into long slices
1 large onion, peeled and diced
olive oil, for frying
1 garlic clove, peeled and chopped
1 tsp ground cumin
1 × 400g tin chopped tomatoes
small bunch fresh coriander (optional)
small bunch fresh parsley (optional)
4 large eggs
100g feta (optional)
bread, for dunking

Method

1. Add the peppers and onion to an oiled frying pan and cook over a medium heat to soften them. Add in your garlic and cumin and cook for a further couple of minutes.
2. Stir in the chopped tomatoes and cook for a few more minutes. At this point, add in the coriander and parsley, if using, and leave to simmer over a low heat for up to 5 minutes.
3. Next, use a wooden spoon to make four gaps in your sauce. Then, crack an egg into each one. Once the eggs are in, pop a lid on the pan and leave it to cook over a low heat until the egg whites have set but the yolks are still runny.
4. Sprinkle the finished dish with crumbled feta, if using. You can serve this still in the pan, and just dunk bread into it, or decant onto individual plates.

Courgetti

A lovely, easy recipe my parents taught me, which is a great fusion of vegetables and pasta. It's also a *very* quick meal with minimal prep (or brain power) required, so great for when you're in a bit of a rush.

What you need
1 courgette
olive oil, for frying
1 garlic clove, peeled and chopped
150g prawns (optional)
2 tbsp pine nuts (optional)
150g edamame beans or peas (optional)
250g gnocchi
jar of pesto

Method
1. Cut up your courgettes into long slices (cut in half, then half again, and chop into batons).
2. Oil a pan and fry the courgettes with the garlic. If you want to add prawns, pine nuts and edamame beans or peas, add these now, too.
3. Bring a saucepan of salted water to the boil and add in your gnocchi (this takes about 2 minutes to cook).
4. Once cooked and drained, add the gnocchi to the frying pan and mix in enough pesto to coat everything. Serve and enjoy!

Bulk Chicken Sandwich Filling

To avoid having to make lunch every day, I just cook up a big batch of this. It was recommended to me by my friend John, a personal trainer, as it is full of protein and can be added to wholemeal bread rolls or wraps with fresh salad, then shoved in a lunch box for a library snack.

What you need
4 chicken breasts
1 x 400g jar of butter chicken or BBQ sauce
1 tsp paprika
salt and pepper, to taste

Method
1. Preheat the oven to 180°C/350°F/Gas 4.
2. Dice the chicken breasts into bite-sized pieces. (Always wash your hands after handling raw chicken.)
3. Put the chicken in a baking tray or dish, then season with paprika, salt and pepper, and mix it around to make sure the seasoning is evenly distributed. Bake in the oven for 15–20 minutes.
4. Remove from the oven and pour over a jar of butter chicken or BBQ sauce, then return the dish to the oven.

5. Cook for another 10–15 minutes until the chicken is cooked right through and piping hot.*
6. Remove from the oven, allow to cool, then put all of the chicken and sauce into a bowl or Tupperware. Once completely cooled, cover and pop it in the fridge.
7. Scoop out some chicken into a sandwich or wrap with lettuce and tomato for a perfect lunch.

A Super-easy Soy Glaze

This is one of the easiest glazes to make for chicken or fish and will leave your taste buds dancing like Anton du Beke. I absolutely swear by this whenever I make a fillet of salmon with rice, and if it's so idiot-proof that I can do it, then you can, too.

What you need
2 tbsp soy sauce
1 tbsp honey
½ garlic clove, crushed

Method
1. Put all the ingredients into a ramekin or small bowl and mix together with a fork.
2. Pour three-quarters of the mix over your meat or fish as it cooks, then add the final quarter afterwards.

---

* Undercooked chicken can give you food poisoning, so make sure it is fully cooked through and piping hot before serving.

Cheap and easy vegan cooking

I've drafted in the WONDERFUL Ruby Granger – an incredible YouTuber and student at Exeter University – to share her very best vegan cooking tips and her favourite vegan recipe.

Vegan Cooking Tips

1. Buy tinned pulses and beans in bulk. These are a cheap and easy way to get protein, and you can add them to pretty much any dish.
2. Spinach is *amazing*. If you buy it frozen, it can be really affordable, and you can then add it to pretty much any meal.
3. Things like spices, tahini and nutritional yeast are great to keep in the cupboard. They last a really long time and add masses of flavour to a dish.
4. Plan ahead! If you're vegan, you probably eat lots of fresh fruits and veggies, and these will easily go off if you're not careful. At the beginning of the week, plan your meals and make sure you'll actually be using up the fresh produce you buy.

Super-easy Couscous Tagine (vegan)

What you need

200g wholegrain couscous

½ white onion, peeled and diced

2 garlic cloves, peeled and chopped

1 tsp olive oil

½ × 400g tin chopped tomatoes

1 tbsp tahini (optional)

1 tsp turmeric

Method

1. Cook the couscous as per the packet instructions.
2. In a frying pan, sauté the onion and garlic in the oil, using water to deglaze the pan as needed.
3. Once the onion is translucent, add the chopped tomatoes, tahini, if using, and turmeric. Add the cooked couscous, mix everything together and serve.

Cooking Eggs Six Ways

This is your ultimate guide to cooking up an egg-cellent meal, in six cracking ways. Seriously, cooking eggs is no yolk, and it's worth taking the time to teach yourself now. I'm eggcited to be going on this journey with you. So, don't be a chicken – give them a go!

How do you like your eggs in the morning ...?

Fried Egg: Oil a frying pan and crack your egg into it without splitting the yolk. To crack the egg, in what can only be referred to as cracking style, tap it against a hard surface to make a clean, horizontal split, then pull the shell apart with your thumbs, pulling up and away, without letting any of the shell fall into the pan. Once the egg starts frying, add some salt and pepper on top for added flavour. Flip it over using a spatula for sunny-side down (meaning both sides are fried) or just keep it sunny-side up (so the yolk is runny).

Poached Egg: Bring a saucepan of water to the boil. Crack each egg into an individual bowl or ramekin. Next, swirl the water into a vortex using a spoon and drop an egg into the centre. Leave the egg to cook for 4½ minutes, then fish it out using a slotted spoon. If you want to do multiple eggs at once, don't worry about swirling the water, just use a spoon to push the whispy egg whites back towards the poached egg.

Scrambled Egg: Oil a pan and add 3 cracked eggs with a knob of butter. Cook over a low heat until starting to set around the edge – remember, it's a marathon not a sprint so don't rush it. Whisk the eggs (this is the *scrambling* bit), then season to taste with salt and pepper. Finally, put a lid on the pan for a couple of minutes (off the heat) to make your scrambled egg nice and fluffy.

Boiled Eggs: Lower your egg(s) into a saucepan of boiling water one at a time using a spoon, then leave it to boil away. For a soft-boiled egg (still runny), leave it for 5½ minutes; for semi-soft, 7½ minutes; for hard-boiled (not runny), up to 12 minutes. Once you've got your timing perfect, you're on to a winner. Top tip: add a little pinch of salt to the boiling water to minimise the chance of the eggs cracking.

Omelette: Now you've got the basics, it's time to really egg-cell yourself with a super-easy recipe. Omelettin' you in on a secret, this is one of the cheapest and easiest recipes for feeding yourself. Heat an oiled frying pan over a medium heat and whisk up your eggs (I'd recommend 3 per person) in a bowl. Tip into the pan and mix around for the first 30 seconds, making sure to fill any gaps with runny egg. After this, leave the egg alone and allow it cook for a couple of minutes until it's begun to set. Add cheese and other toppings of your choice (pre-cooked if necessary) at this stage. Once the omelette has cooked enough to hold its shape, use a spatula to flip one half over. Finally, serve it up and enjoy.

Frittata (serves 2): I hope you're not eggshausted yet ... here's one final way to cook eggs. A frittata is kind of like a big omelette or a quiche without the crusts. Preheat the oven to 200°C/400°F/Gas 6. Crack 6 eggs into a bowl and whisk them up – don't be too forceful, though, or you'll splash it onto your clothes ... it's whisky business. Then pick your toppings. I like to go for feta and spinach, but chorizo and potato (pre-cooked) is another great mix. Chop up your toppings into small chunks and tip them into your egg mixture. Next, pour the mixture into an ovenproof pan and bake in the oven for 15–20 minutes. Remove the pan from the oven when the egg is cooked all the way through (run a knife through the middle to check).

(Tip: If you're not sure if your eggs are okay to eat, here's an easy way to check. Fill a glass of water and add the suspicious egg in question. If the egg sinks to the bottom, it's good to eat; if it lays flat on its side, it's very fresh. If, however, the egg floats to the surface, it's gone off.)

CHAPTER 5

SOCIAL

One of the most integral, enriching parts of university is the social life. Getting involved in clubs and societies is a fantastic way to make friends – you're likely to have lots in common with the people who join the same ones as you, since you have a clearly stated shared passion. You've got your first ice-breaker out of the way, at least, as you already know you both have an interest in what you're doing. Throwing yourself into extra-curricular activities is also the perfect chance to learn a new skill or find a new hobby. And on top of that, there's all the socials and fancy-dress parties that will soon be crammed into your diary. Your social life will be a huuuuge part of your university experience, so make like Tom Daley and dive in.

Clubs and societies

Generally speaking, the word club refers to sports teams, while society applies to all the other things you could possibly have a passion for: from law and politics to hummus or Colin Firth (or all of the above).

Clubs and societies will often organise 'socials' – which are just gatherings – that consist of lunches, hang-outs, bar crawls, etc. You'll meet so many fascinating people across year groups at these events who you wouldn't normally have the opportunity to cross paths with, so embrace this opportunity and meet some new people.

University is probably one of the best opportunities to pick up a brand-new sport, when you'll have the time to do it, so why not give it a go? I started playing mixed lacrosse in the second year of my degree as a complete beginner, and it was great fun (even though I had to be sin-binned within five minutes of my first ever game ... no one actually taught me the rules). You could learn a new language, improve your creative writing, debate interesting political views you've never been exposed to before, and so on.

I remember being told at the beginning of my time at university: 'Don't let your degree get in the way of your education.' As profound, righteous and a bit clichéd as that may sound, it's actually very true. Part of the education you receive at university is through clubs and societies, and you'll look back on your involvement with fond memories. I've met incredible people, been introduced to wildly diverse world views and opinions, found new passions and honed my craft in things I already loved, and I will be incredibly sad to move on from university and leave all of this behind.

Starting your own society

If the club or society you want to be part of doesn't exist, or none of the societies on offer represent your specialist interest, then make it yourself. You usually need a minimum number of founding members and the patience of a saint to go through all the paperwork (and deal with university bureaucracy) in order to be ratified, but this will vary depending on the uni. Check your Students' Union website to find out exactly how to do this, and what their requirements are. The admin at the beginning will be so worth it in the end when you can enjoy the Strongbow Dark Fruits of your labour.

Societies you didn't know existed, but will now want to join ...

- Hummus Society (Durham)
- David Attenborough Society (Winchester)
- IKEA Appreciation Society (Bristol)
- Eurovison Society (Birmingham)
- Pun Society (Sussex)
- Shrek Society (Glasgow)
- Battle Re-enactment Society (Liverpool)
- Meme Society (Northumbria)
- Chicken Wing Society (Glasgow)
- Tiddlywinks Society (Cambridge)
- Stitch 'n' Bitch Society (Leeds)
- Stationery Society (Sheffield)
- Louis Theroux Society (Birmingham)
- Broke Society (UCL)
- Kettle Society (Nottingham)
- Cider Society (Bournemouth)
- Bell-ringing Society (Birmingham)
- Tetris Society (Durham)
- Robot Football (Plymouth)
- Humans vs Zombies (Royal Holloway)
- Garlic Bread Society (UEA)
- Gregorian Chant Society (Oxford)

- Dog-walking Society (Sussex)
- Doctor Who Society (Warwick)
- Custard-wrestling Society (Cardiff)
- Kigus (animal onesies) Society (York)
- Danny DeVito Society (York)
- Hot-air Balloon Society (Strathclyde)
- Howling Society (Aberystwyth)
- Fetish Society (Lincoln)
- 20-minute Society (Newcastle)
- Beer Pong Society (Portsmouth)
- *Mario Kart* Society (Essex)
- Pooh Sticks Society (Cambridge)
- Extreme Ironing Society (Nottingham)
- Guild of Assassins (Staffordshire)
- BBQ on a Sunday Society (Liverpool)
- Cheese and Wine Society (Cardiff)
- Buffy the Vampire Slayer Society (Sussex)
- Pudding-eating Society (Winchester)
- Quidditch Society (Belfast)
- Sheila and Her Dog Society (Cambridge)
- Viking Society (Plymouth)
- Bad Film Society (Birmingham)
- Octopush – Underwater Hockey (Oxford)
- Taylor Swift Society (Durham)
- Kids' Party Games – Hide and Soc. (Nottingham)
- *Pokémon* Society (Leeds)
- RuneScape (Birmingham)
- Brutalist Society (Oxford)

- Curry Society (Leicester)
- Knit Like Your Nanna (Sheffield Hallam)
- Beekeeping Society (Southampton)
- Gastrointestinal Society (Liverpool)
- Colin Firth Appreciation Society (Durham)

(Note: As wonderful as all of these sound, make sure you've checked on your Students' Union website that they're still running at the time you're reading this. They all existed in 2020 when I compiled this list!)

How to get involved in clubs and societies

Freshers' Fair is a great way to find out about all these different clubs and societies ~~and grab a bucket load of freebies as you go~~ and chat to the people who run them. Sign up for anything that sounds remotely interesting or appealing, especially as most groups will have a 'taster' preview session. It's also a good idea to sign up to mailing lists and join Facebook groups so you know what events are being hosted.

If you miss the Freshers' Fair, or you're halfway through term two and feeling a bit bored, check out the Students' Union website for a full breakdown and description of all the clubs and societies they have to offer. You can join a club or society at any time, not just at the beginning of the year.

Also, remember that there are other places to find activities to get involved with, rather than just those exclusive to the university. For sports, perhaps consider joining a local team, and meet some people from the area you're living in. There may also be some volunteering opportunities in the local area that you can get involved with, particularly in local schools or charities. For the former you'll need a Disclosure and Barring Service (DBS) check, but usually your uni will be able to facilitate this.*

---

* DBS forms are notoriously slow to be approved. So if you're already thinking you'll want to do some voluntary (or paid) work that will require one, get ahead of the game and complete the DBS check in advance.

You could even consider running for a role on a club or society's executive committee, as they cannot operate without students to lead them. Usually positions include president, vice president, treasurer, social secretary and more. Running for these roles will give you experience in public speaking and filling in applications, as well as organising events or managing the financial side of a club, meaning they look great on your CV.

Surviving your first social

You've joined the clubs or societies you found most appealing and have attended your first few sessions. Now it's time for the best bit … the social. A social is essentially an event that gets everyone with a common interest together to hang out, chill and get to know one another. More often than not, they will take place in a bar or restaurant, as they're the largest social spaces available. There's usually a detailed dress code, elaborate games and a really great atmosphere. Your first social will certainly be a baptism of fire for your university experience, so here's my ultimate survival guide, as someone who has also been the social secretary for many societies (most notably, Durham University's Hummus Society) …

1. **Dress codes:** They're set for a reason, and you will be expected to uphold them. No matter how silly you *think* you look, you'll look far sillier if you don't make an effort and everyone else does. Not only is fancy dress a great way to identify other people on your social, it's also the best conversation starter of all time. Complimenting someone else's costume is the easiest way of breaking the ice, and you'll probably come across as more of a fun person the more effort you put in. Be creative with it, and remember, you don't always need to buy something in order to make a great costume. I realised there was a 'dress as something

beginning with the first letter of your name' dress code about 20 minutes before leaving for a social once, and managed to quickly make a jellyfish costume using bubble-wrap, tape and a pink T-shirt I had lying around in about 4 minutes.* I swear, it's doable!

2. **Feeling comfortable:** Universities now have very strict measures in place to ensure that clubs and societies aren't pressuring anyone to do anything they don't want to do, making a safe, inclusive, welcoming environment for everyone. Most have banned 'initiations' (although these are now commonly disguised by the less intimidating words 'welcome drinks'), and clubs/societies that are caught out will face severe consequences. You are absolutely allowed to say no if you don't want to do a certain game or challenge. If you aren't comfortable then you don't have to do it, and everyone should (and will) respect that. As someone who has been social sec. of a club, if someone said they didn't want to participate, that was

---

* In case you were wondering (although I'm pretty certain no one was), the way to do this is as follows: 1) Put on the pink T-shirt. 2) Cut out two vest-shaped pieces of bubble-wrap, measured up to your body. 3) Tape the two bubble-wrap vests together at the shoulders. 4) Put this over your head. 5) Tape the two bubble-wrap vests together at the hips/waist now that it's on your body (it'll be kind of like the shape of a netball bib). 6) Cut out strips of bubble-wrap to be your tentacles. 7) Tape the bubble-wrap tentacles to the bottom of your bubble-wrap vest, front and back. 8) Live your best jellyfish life and receive many compliments while doing so.

absolutely fine – I wanted everyone to have the most fun possible. You don't have to justify yourself to anyone, and everyone will have forgotten about it in two minutes flat. If they are persistent or somewhat forceful, it probably doesn't come from a malicious place; it just comes from them wanting everyone to be involved and able to let themselves go. However, nothing is binding, and no one can enforce any rules you aren't comfortable with. So say no if you're not sure, and also back up anyone else who ever decides to take a time out, even if it's something you're participating in. Have each other's backs, because it'll be way better for everyone. If you are made to feel uncomfortable despite saying no, take it up with your Students' Union so they can continue to make it a safer environment for everyone.

3. **Drinking alcohol is ALWAYS optional:** Inevitably, a lot of socials will involve drinking in some capacity, or at least take place in a bar. However, there is absolutely no obligation to drink alcohol. Soft drinks can replace alcohol in pretty much any drinking game, so you can still participate – plus, downing a pint of fizzy lemonade is waaaay more impressive than a pint of beer. For instance, a popular game at socials I've been to is what's called Boat Race. Basically, everyone grabs an alcopop in a bottle and stands in two lines. The person at the front starts drinking and the person

behind them can only start drinking once the person in front has an empty bottle. The first line to complete the drinking relay wins. Alcohol is not necessary for this, though. Replace the alcopop with a J2O and it literally makes no difference: the challenge is still the same. Drink alcohol if you feel comfortable, don't drink alcohol if you don't want to, and be fair to yourself and others.

4. **Say hello to everyone:** If you're part of a club or society then that means you have an interest in the area it covers, and so will everyone else who's part of it. Socials are the ideal opportunity to meet like-minded people, and you already have the first hurdle (of working out what to chat about) sorted: talk about the club or society, why they chose to join and how long they've been part of it. This is one of the best ways to make friends, so don't be afraid to go to socials alone. Everyone will be in the mood for chatting, so don't be shy and make the first move.

Easy ice-breakers

- *Ask someone how long they've been part of the society. This will probably give you an idea of what year group they're in, which you can also discuss. If they've been a member for ages, you can ask what their experience has been. If they've just joined, like you, then there's solidarity in both being newbies.*

- *Ask about people's interest in the subject area the society covers and talk about your individual experience with it. Everyone there has a common passion, so it's a great way of putting yourselves on a level playing field.*

- *Ask about people's backgrounds – where they're from; whether they took a gap year; what A Levels they took; whether they have pets (always the easiest way to get someone interested); what they study; where they live; how many people they live with; how they're finding the workload; what other societies they're a member of, etc.*

Social theme ideas

If you're organising a night out at uni for a large group of people, you need a theme – and the more elaborate, the more memorable. Here's some inspo!

(Note: All games can use either alcoholic or non-alcoholic beverages. It's your choice, so do whatever you're most comfortable with.)

1. ***Où est le poulet?*:** Everyone gets into (or is put into) pairs and puts a fiver into a pot. Then every pair is put into a random generator (you can find these online) or use a hat and one is selected. These people become *'le poulet'* (the chicken), preferably with chicken costumes provided. They then have 15 minutes to secretly run to any bar in the city and start spending the kitty money on drinks. After those 15 minutes are up, all the other pairs set off to try to find the chickens ... and the drink money. Every bar you go into, you have to buy a drink, and you can only leave once you've finished it. If the chickens aren't there, get your drink, down it, and go on to the next one. Once you walk into the correct bar and spot the chickens, you can start spending the kitty money, too. Everyone who finds the chickens starts drinking using the communal pot of money and stays in the bar, until either the cash stash is depleted or the

last people turn up – whichever happens first. This is a great way to explore more bars in your uni city and also get to know your partner really well.

2. **Tied social:** Again, this one involves being paired up and getting to know your partner pretty well ... except this time even more intimately. Pairs are tied together, either by their wrists or legs, and have to spend the whole night as one entity. This is particularly good when two clubs join forces for a social – for example, netball and rugby teams, or the university Labour and Conservative societies. I don't know which one would be more chaotic.

3. **Pub golf:** This is essentially a bar crawl where each pub is like a golf hole: it has a par. This means that each one has a number of sips you're allowed to finish your drink in. If the par is three, get a drink you can finish in three gulps. If it's one, get a shot – or a pint if you really back yourself. Basically, this means you need to know your own limits and be able to judge what size of drink you should get for each par. Alternatively, buy each other's drinks and challenge each other. You can make a score sheet to keep track of how everyone is doing, or just take it easy – either is good fun.

4. **Lock-in:** This is one for when you don't want to go to a pub or restaurant, and fancy just chilling at someone's house. Everyone goes to the shops and buys some drinks (and probably some snacks) and then, once everyone has arrived, no one can leave until every drink is finished. This often results in an all-nighter, and is particularly good when you've just finished a big project together – for example, if you're the cast of a play, or were volunteering at Freshers' Week – and want to celebrate as a group.

5. **Head to head:** Tell everyone to come according to either one dress code or another – for example, ninjas versus pirates. Half the people come as ninjas, half the people come as pirates. Then, on the night, these are the two teams who go head to head in all the challenges and games. Often, the freshers are given the more compromising costume – for instance, gods and goddesses versus grapes in which freshers become the fruity latter. It's a rite of passage.

Costume ideas

Trying to find a costume to wear on a university night out can be time-consuming. So, I decided to save you the endless Pinterest searching with a handy list of 112 (yes, ONE HUNDRED AND TWELVE) costume ideas. I worked out that my academic year consists of 194 days at university, so surely you can't possibly need any more inspiration than this ...

For one person

1. The Black Eyed Peas (colour your eyes in black)
2. A formal apology (dress up in fancy business-wear and hold up a sign saying 'Sorry')
3. Cereal killer (stab a box of cereal – preferably with a plastic knife)
4. Identity theft (steal your friends' IDs and stick them to yourself)
5. A bag of M&M's (cover yourself in pictures of the rapper Eminem)
6. Nudist on strike (just don't wear a costume)
7. *50 Shades of Grey* (just wear loads of shades of grey)
8. Bread winner (a loaf of bread and a medal)
9. Blessing in disguise (fake glasses/moustache and a T-shirt with the word 'Blessing' on it)
10. One-night stand (carry your bedside table – just one – with you)

11. An olive (*Angus, Thongs and Perfect Snogging* inspired)
12. 'When life gives you lemons' (wear a T-shirt that says 'LIFE' on it and dish out lemons all evening)
13. Ceiling fan (dress like a cheerleader with a sign that says I ♥ THE CEILING)
14. Holy guacamole (think angel meets avocado)
15. Smart cookie (graduation cap and gown, and a pack of Marylands)
16. *The Devil Wears Prada* (classic devil outfit plus T-shirt that says 'Prada' on it)
17. Facebook (tape a book to your face)
18. Insta-gran (grandma props at the ready ... you're an instant grandmother)
19. Post Malone (draw on all of his tattoos ... just make sure the pen isn't permanent and won't still be there in tomorrow's lecture)

For duos

1. Netflix and chill
2. Salt and pepper
3. Mario and Luigi
4. Barbie and Ken
5. Thing 1 and Thing 2
6. Mermaid Man and Barnacle Boy
7. Minnie and Mickey Mouse
8. Rick and Morty
9. Two boobs

10. #NoFilter and #Filter
11. Spongebob and Patrick
12. Rum and coke
13. Gin and tonic
14. Double denim
15. Harley Quinn and the Joker
16. Political enemies
17. Coleen Rooney and ... it's Rebekah Vardy's account
18. Your favourite *X Factor* contestants
19. Sherlock and Dr Watson
20. Phineas and Ferb
21. Ben and Jerry
22. Wine and cheese
23. *The Fairly Odd Parents*
24. Fiona and Shrek

For groups

1. Crayons
2. Army/camo
3. Tennis players
4. Devils
5. Angels
6. Wizards/*Harry Potter*
7. Cowboys
8. The *Scooby-Doo* gang
9. *The Incredibles*
10. Safari animals

11. Princes/Princesses

12. Social-media apps

13. *Mario Kart*

14. *The Flintstones*

15. *Pokémon*

16. Fruit salad

17. Superheroes

18. *Orange Is the New Black*

19. Jocks and cheerleaders

20. Rainbow (the TV programme *or* the colours)

21. Shark Week

22. *The Sims*

23. Cards Against Humanity

24. Doctors

25. Pirates

26. Lifeguards

27. Oompa-Loompas

28. Spice Girls

29. A famous band

30. *Ghostbusters*

31. Gangsters/*Peaky Blinders*

32. The Olympic rings

33. N-Dubz

34. Pints of beer

35. Quality Streets

36. Tequila, lime and salt

37. Rock, Paper, Scissors

38. *The Simpsons*

39. *Inside Out*

40. Winnie-the-Pooh

41. *Mean Girls*

42. *Grease*

43. Fizzy drinks

44. *Toy Story* aliens

45. Dominoes (the game or pizza)

46. The four elements

47. Pac-Man ghosts

48. *I'm a Celebrity ...* contestants

49. Fruit

Party themes

1. M&S vs S&M (dressing gowns vs lingerie)

2. Anything but clothes (think binbags or Twister mats)

3. *The Great Gatsby* (1920s speakeasy vibes)

4. Shaken, not stirred (James Bond/casino black-tie)

5. Jobs you dreamed of as a child

6. Back to school (shudder)

7. Dress as your subject

8. Sixties, Seventies, Eighties, Nineties or Noughties

9. Murder mystery (Cluedo vibes)

10. Silent disco

11. Grammys/Oscars after-party

12. White T-shirts (with lots of pens to write on each other with)

13. Post-apocalypse (zombies)

14. Internet memes (unleash the Vine references)
15. Dress as something beginning with the first letter of your name
16. Pyjama party (what we all dreamed of as a kid)
17. Tight and bright (neon, vibrant and the tighter the better)
18. Ugly jumper party (particularly good at Christmas)
19. You are what you eat (dress as your favourite food)
20. Dynamic duos (see earlier list)

Group games

Ever get halfway through a social event and feel the need to spice it up a little bit? Well, I'm here with three years' experience of university to provide some ideas for organised fun:

- **Biggest regret at uni so far:** *This one's pretty self-explanatory, but I'll cover the basics anyway. Go round the circle and confess your biggest regret of uni so far. Get it? Got it? Good.*

- **'If I get the highest number ...':** *Write out loads of different numbers on separate pieces of paper. Each person stands up, announces 'If I get the highest number, I will ...' and then names a forfeit (examples include dying their hair, getting a tattoo or pouring a drink over themselves). They then pull a piece of paper out of the hat, lick the back and stick it to their forehead so everyone else can see the number. Then the hat is passed on to the next person, who repeats the process until everyone has done it and it's clear who has to do their forfeit.*

- **Arrogance:** *All you need for this is a selection of drinks, a cup and a coin. When the glass is passed to you, pour in an amount of your chosen drink, depending on how confident you are that you'll be able to correctly guess* whether a flipped coin lands on heads or tails. Make your prediction, flip the coin, and if you're right, pass on the cup to the next person, who repeats the process. If you're wrong, down the drink, then add in more and flip again until you get it right. If everyone keeps predicting correctly, the drink becomes what's known as a 'dirty pint' (aka a grim concoction of different drinks; the cocktail absolutely no one wants). If you're feeling arrogant then add a lot of drink to the cup, because it won't be you having to drink it.

- **Palm Tree:** For this one, you need a cup and some playing cards. Place the cup in the middle of the group, with each person pouring a bit of their drink into it. Then each person takes it in turn to balance a card on top of the cup, with each card having to overlap and sitting further out than the last. Take it in turns to keep adding cards in a circular shape around the cup's rim – it'll start to resemble a palm tree sort of shape – until someone's card makes the whole thing collapse. It's sort of like a student version of Buckaroo.

- **Cardboard Game:** Reuse a big piece of cardboard from an old box and collapse it so that it's flat. Grab a marker pen and write every player's name around the edge, before drawing a circle around each name. Then go round the circle and take it in turns to flip a coin onto the cardboard. If you land on someone's name, that person has to down their drink (or just take a sip). If you land on a blank piece of the cardboard, write a new rule and then draw a circle around it. If anyone then lands in that circle, they have to do the rule or forfeit.

- **'Is it awkward that ...?':** *This is a quick-fire question game. You start by saying someone's name and then ask them a question led by, 'Is it awkward that ...?' – probably bringing up some inside jokes or home truths. Instead of answering, the person asked fires back another 'Is it awkward that ...?' at someone else (anyone aside from the person who last asked). If someone stutters, can't think of a question, is tripped up by the question or doesn't bounce back quickly enough, they have to either answer the question or drink.*

- **'Never have I ever ...':** *The classic. Each person declares a statement starting with 'Never have I ever ...' – drink if you have, don't drink if you haven't. An additional element is that the last person to drink has to explain the context of why they have done that thing.*

- **Back to Back:** *Two people stand back to back with a drink in hand. The other people in the room shout questions at them, along the general lines of 'Who is most likely to ...?' Examples would be: Who's better dressed? Who's going to throw up tonight? Who's most likely to say 'I love you' and not mean it? Who's most* *likely to have had an STI? Go in as hard as possible – the more outrageous the better. If they think the question applies to them, and they're the most likely, then they drink. If both people drink, or neither drink, then the forfeit is that they both have to drink again. If only one person drinks, and the pair therefore agree on who is the most likely, then everyone else in the room has to drink. Once they agree on three things, they swap out for someone else.*

- **3, 2, 1:** *Similar to Back to Back, but with three people standing in a line with their backs to the room. Each person is assigned a number: three, two or one. When the 'Who is most likely …?' questions are asked by everyone else in the room, the three people vote behind their backs by holding up either 1, 2 or 3 fingers. They do this behind their backs so they can't see who the others voted for but everyone else in the room can. If they all agree, the room drinks; if they disagree, the contestants drink.*

- **Fuzzy Duck:** *Go round the room clockwise, with each person saying 'fuzzy duck' in turn, the quicker the better. If someone says 'duzzy' the direction changes, and you say 'ducky fuzz' instead. When someone else says 'duzzy' it changes direction back to 'fuzzy duck'. If someone messes it up and says the wrong thing, they have to drink. Don't get why this is funny yet? Give the game a go and* *you'll soon see why messing it up causes the whole room to giggle.*

- **Ring of Fire:** *Spread a pack of cards face-down around an empty glass. Each person picks up a card and has to do a rule based on the number on the card. Ace = waterfall (everyone starts drinking and you can only stop once the person before you does); 2 = you (pick someone else to drink); 3 = me (you have to drink); 4 = girls drink; 5 = thumbs (everyone has to put their thumb on the table; the last person to do so drinks); 6 = boys drink; 7 = heaven (everyone has to point upwards; the last person to do so drinks); 8 = mate (pick a drinking partner who now has to drink any time you do); 9 = rhyme (say a word and everyone goes round the circle saying a word that rhymes with it until someone repeats a word or can't think of one, and they have to drink); 10 = categories (name a category, such as types of hat, beer brands, dog breeds or ice-cream flavours, and everyone names something in that category – the first person who repeats or can't think of one has to drink); Jack = make a new rule (for example, not drinking with your dominant hand, not being able to use anyone's first names, not being able to point, etc.); Queen = question master (you fire questions at people in the group – if anyone answers, they have to drink); King = pour some of your drink into the cup in the middle; the person who picks up the last King has to finish the drink.*

CHAPTER 6

LIFE

University life is such a surreal and bonkers experience. It's like another world, where you just embrace the madness and stop questioning it when you see four people dressed as Teletubbies queuing for an ATM outside a bar. Pulling an all-nighter doesn't feel like a stupid decision when there are no parents to tell you to go to bed, and eating your spaghetti hoops out of the saucepan isn't frowned upon – it saves washing up!! I always find it funny how, during term, you never really leave university – even when you go to your student house, you're still in that uni bubble.

In this section, I want to address some of the other elements of university life, from student finance to studying abroad. I've also interviewed some very interesting people to hear their views, too, as I'm sure you're sick of me by now.

How does student finance work?

When you apply to university, you will need to tell them how you're intending to pay for the degree. For most of us, the answer won't be cash or card – we need a bit of extra funding to get us through. Make sure you've checked when the deadline for applying for this is, though, as you don't want to end up in a sticky situation.

So, how do student loans work? Well, the government will lend you money to fund your degree, which you pay back once you've graduated. You only begin paying this back when your income is more than £25,725 a year, and repayments are set at 9 per cent of everything you earn above £25,725.* There's a staggering interest rate, too, but anything not repaid in 30 years is written off completely.

A loan declaration will appear in the post roughly six weeks after you submit your application, and this will confirm how much you'll be receiving. Student Finance usually pay the money into your account a couple of days before each term starts, and it's the ultimate sext seeing the words 'Your money will arrive in your bank account within three working days'.

---

* For example, if you earn £30,000 one year, that is £4,275 over the threshold; 9 per cent of that £4,275 would be paid back to Student Finance, so you would pay £384.75 that year.

Tuition Fee Loan: This just covers your tuition fees and is paid from Student Finance straight to the university. You never see this money, as it's never paid directly to you. This loan can range all the way up to the maximum tuition fee (for example, it is currently £9,250 a year in England).

Maintenance Loan: This covers your living costs, from food and rent to books and stationery – everything you need to maintain yourself while you do your degree. The size of this loan depends on your household income, as the assumption is that you or your family will provide the rest of the money you need to survive.

Grants and scholarships

If there's one thing we know, it's that universities have a metric shit-tonne of money. They're rolling in it. I imagine a pro vice-chancellor to live their life like a rapper in an R&B music video, with a bathtub full of £10 notes and a diamond-encrusted gravy boat adorning their silk-clothed dining table.*

This means that they're often willing to give money to students they can support. Unfortunately, all too often students don't even realise the opportunities are there. A ridiculous number of scholarships and grants go to waste because no one claims them, when actually loads of people are eligible to apply.

It's difficult to explain exactly what your next steps should be, as it's different for every individual (based on your circumstances and institution), but I can share a little insight at least. Scholarships and grants are often given out to a) those who are being recognised for academic achievement; b) those from disadvantaged backgrounds; c) those who wish to travel for educational purposes; d) people who benefit the university by generating good press. Essentially, you're a marketing tool for the university as well as a way of filling up an accessibility quota, and a scholarship or grant is their way of supporting you.

---

* Upon reading this back, I'm not 100 per cent sure that many R&B music videos include gravy boats as props, but I would like to see it.

This free money is usually given out on a case-by-case basis, especially for those using it to facilitate travel. If you can justify why some extra cash for travelling would really help you out, often there are grants and scholarships that are willing to offer you some money in exchange for a short write-up they can use to show how they're supporting their students. Whether you end up with a £10 donation or an all-expenses-paid trip, you never know unless you apply.

Many universities will have awards with cash prizes, donated by former students who now earn big, big dollars, as well as ex-employees and trustees. However, they won't seek you out and just send you a random cheque; they'll want you to apply and explain why you should be nominated for it. Sure, you may have to jump through a few hoops to receive it, but you've got to do what you've got to do to secure the bag.

University summers and what to do with them

University summers are long and, after the initial excitement of being back home with your family pets, you'll probably find yourself twiddling your thumbs wondering what to do. It's the perfect opportunity to do something amazing, so here's some suggestions …

Top tips for student travel

1. Look for volunteering opportunities abroad, which make the trip cheaper! Last summer, I travelled to China and taught English in Shenzhen with fellow university students – and all I had to pay for were my flights and visa. I made awesome friends, had an incredible experience and explored a beautiful country, while also securing a TEFL qualification! I found out about this through a company called Gotoco, who attended Freshers' Fair, but I'm sure there are hundreds of other opportunities all around the world with various volunteering or 'cultural exchange' schemes.

2. Use Skyscanner to find cheap flights. If you just want to travel and don't necessarily want to work, keep an eye on some cheeky deals. Skyscanner basically spot the

best prices so you don't have to and have all the flight details you could ever need to know. If you're not fussy about where you go, there's an option to check the cheapest flights from the UK to anywhere – just type in 'everywhere' in the destination bar. There are also alternative cheap flight finders like Jack's Flight Club (nothing to do with me, I swear) and Scott's Cheap Flights, which spot flash deals and send them straight to your email inbox.

3. Get a travel card like Monzo or Revolut, which can be used abroad with no additional costs. Getting your card blocked by the bank when you're abroad is a nightmare – *trust me* – so don't get caught out. Also, if you're pretty prone to losing things and are constantly playing a game of Where's Wally? with ALL of your possessions then one feature of these cards is particularly appealing. You can 'freeze' your card if you misplace it, so that if it has been stolen, no one can use it. Then, when you inevitably find it lodged in a shoe or stuck to your sun-cream bottle, you can just 'defrost' the card and start using it again, without ever cancelling it outright. Because that's a faff and can leave you sleeping on the floor of Singapore's Changi Airport without access to any money, meaning you can't even buy yourself a sandwich or a bottle of water ... unless you're my mum reading this, in which case, that never happened to me.

4. Packing cubes are great for compartmentalising your bag. Big travelling backpacks are pretty tricky to a) pack and b) unpack, and suddenly finding your last pair of underwear is like searching for a needle in a haystack. Packing cubes help to separate all of your things, so you can have one zip-bag for T-shirts, and another for underwear, or a bag for clean clothes and another bag for dirty ones. These are available on Amazon.

5. Don't be afraid of hostels. I stay in hostels absolutely everywhere I go – including when I travel around the UK. They are great places to meet like-minded people and are ridiculously cheap, often in central locations. The best deal I've ever managed to find was in Vietnam where a night's stay, a spring-roll-making class, an hour of free breakfast and rum and coke were all included in the price of ... wait for it ... £3. THREE POUNDS. That's Beyoncé-featuring-CRAY-Z. I usually find these using the app Hostelworld, where previous visitors leave insightful reviews. If you'd prefer a bit more privacy then Airbnb is also great.

6. Map.me is a fantastic app where you can download detailed maps of locations in advance and then use (with GPS) when you no longer have Wi-Fi or data. This makes navigating a city a thousand times easier. You can also pinpoint cool locations you want to visit in

advance and save them to the map, so you can try to see everything.

7. Take your student card with you wherever you go because an unbelievable number of attractions all over the world will sort you out with a lovely little discount if you can prove you're a student. Might as well milk it while you can.

Work, work, work, work, work

The summer holiday is also a great opportunity to find work placements and start building up your CV – especially through internships and work experience. These give you practical skills, open your eyes to different jobs that you're qualified for and didn't realise existed and, most importantly, form a connection with a company. Any business is going to be more likely to hire someone after they graduate who they've met before and loved working with, so put in the hours and wow them now to secure a permanent role later down the line. If you can be paid for the work, that's a bonus, too.

You can find student jobs and internships through the careers emails your university sends out or through LinkedIn, Indeed, Debut, Target Connect, Prospect, The Bright Network, Rate My Placement, Graduate Talent Pool and more.

Uni work ...?

Yikes. Someone had to mention it, didn't they? I feel like *that* kid in class who reminds the teacher there was homework due in that they haven't collected yet.

Do a bit of preparatory work for the forthcoming academic year to get yourself ahead of the game, but also remember that you chose that subject for a reason. The holidays are a great time to explore the subject you chose to read for your degree on your own terms, without someone forcing you to take an exam in it in five months' time. Use your new-found wisdom to research things further and explore some new areas you didn't know existed before, and to remind yourself why you chose that degree in the first place. The summer holidays are a great time to rekindle your relationship with your subject – especially after exam season, when it'd be safe to change the status of that relationship to 'It's complicated'. If you're doing a dissertation, this is the perfect opportunity to play the field a bit and find something unusual and enjoyable that you could focus your research project on.

Should you get a job at university?

Listen, none of us wants to be broke at university. It's expensive trying to balance a social life, uni events and, well, feeding yourself, and so some extra dollar is always helpful. Loans never seem to quite cover it and not everyone has unlimited access to the Bank of Mum and Dad, so it may be time to start finding your own source of income. Many students seek employment alongside their degree, and it isn't always glamorous. However, there are some jobs that will suit your needs a lot better, which I'll discuss in this section.

Summer jobs: We've all been there ... working in catering or retail. Work hard and put in the hours over the summer so you don't have to work during the term. Many employers will also allow you to come back during the other holidays – especially at Christmas, when they'll be much keener to hire someone they know and trust rather than a brand-new temporary employee who is bound to require assistance every five minutes and then leave once they finally get the hang of it.

Transfer jobs: See if your employer back home can transfer you to a local store in your university city. Often employers with multiple branches will take on students who can only work seasonal shifts, and then seek other students who can cover when it's term time. Being able to shuffle around and transfer to a different location within the same company saves a whole lot of admin and training, so they'll look favourably on you if you've got the experience down.

Work for student organisations: Often university or student hubs will solely employ students of that university; for example, student bars, uni accommodation or the Students' Union. These employers will be much more understanding of your needs as a student and will have a vested interest in you getting your degree and balancing it alongside your job. If you can't do a shift because of academic commitments, they'll be much more likely to understand and make arrangements for you. Equally, if your colleagues are also students, they'll probably be more flexible when it comes to swapping shifts or covering for you.

Online tutoring: The fact that you're a university student makes you very appealing to pushy parents who want their kids to have some extra tutoring. Often you can find organisations who provide this service online, whether it's for students who need help with GCSEs, A Levels, the IB or general mentoring. You have recently been through those years – and, presumably, you smashed it with flying colours since you're at uni – so you're the perfect candidate to see someone else through it. As long as it doesn't bring you too many flashbacks of past trauma, you should be fine.

Become a student ambassador: Many major brands, like Deliveroo or YouTube Premium, hire students to promote their services on campus and give out freebies. This would be a great way to meet new people, and probably wouldn't be too time-consuming.

Promote something: Gyms, clubs, bars, restaurants, etc. often seek people to hand out flyers in the town centre or outside the Students' Union. So if you're cool with harassing anyone who walks past and waving a leaflet at them like a performer at the Edinburgh Fringe, this'll be right up your street. Just don't be too disheartened when you walk home and spot a big pile of the flyers you gave out in the nearest bin.

Nightclub ticket-selling: Events targeted at students often rely on other students to promote them. This usually means you'll be given more wristbands than a group of Year 12s at the Reading and Leeds Festivals, and the task of trying to flog them. You can offer deals to student groups or socials, encouraging them to buy wristbands from you to guarantee entry into a club.

~~Sell feet pics online:~~ Okay, definitely DON'T do this.

Studying abroad

The opportunity to study abroad is a fantastic one. Unfortunately, this was not something I was able to do, so I've spoken to some people who did in order to share their experiences and valuable insights. Remember, what doesn't deport you makes you stronger ...

What was the biggest cultural shock you experienced?

Naomi (Buenos Aires, Argentina): Argentinians are more friendly, laid-back and open than Brits, late for everything, they eat their bodyweight in red meat and drink mate [a traditional South American caffeine-rich infused drink] like it's water.

Paddy (Taipei, Taiwan): Seeing a language I don't speak on every street sign was really strange. Not being able to order in restaurants, so just having to point and guess. The pace of life I also found really different. People wake up early and sleep early.

Maddey (Canada): I didn't really experience culture shock. I think I had the reverse, where I was surprised by how much of Canadian lifestyle and culture was similar to the UK, in that I didn't really find things that different or strange.

Henry (Paris, France): I was studying at a French university and it was definitely just a completely different university culture. University over there was far more transactional. You go, study and leave. I wasn't used to that and it took a lot of time to acclimatise.

Ellen (Lima, Peru): For me, the biggest cultural shock was the sexism that is so prevalent in Latin America. I couldn't walk down the street without people staring at me or whistling and making comments because I am very blonde and obviously not from Peru. In my first placement, the dad of the family I lived with forbade his wife from working and even though they owned two massive cars, one of which was in her name, only he was allowed to drive them, and he had sole control of the family's finances. This particular case of sexism that I encountered was extreme, but it was important for me to see how some attitudes towards a woman's place in society are so outdated, and while I was not expecting to change an entire country's perception overnight, I did challenge family members who made sexist comments about how women shouldn't work, so they at least heard a different perspective, even if they didn't agree with it.

Jade (San Francisco, US): The lack of British humour! Where's the classic witty sarcasm? The dry banter? The self-deprecating chat about miserable weather or Brexit? Ah, the biggest culture shock was being surrounded by zero Brits. It's meant I've learnt a lot, both about American culture and other cultures from our international students, but it's definitely made me treasure strange parts of British culture that we take for granted!

How would you prepare differently if you could go back?

Paddy (Taipei, Taiwan): I would make three photocopies of every important document I have ever owned. Passport, bank statements, uni enrolment letters – all of it.

Jade (San Francisco, US): Honestly, I'd pack less. It feels counterintuitive, but you just don't need as much as you think you do! Before coming, it's easy to imagine this suitcase holds your entire life, but you can always buy that toothpaste or a pillow or a kettle in-country. I would have been more savage with my packing, especially as you can rely on roommates and flatmates!

Gaby (Paris, France): I think I would look around/ask around more about the different accommodation options. I went for the cheap option of staying in a homestay, but I never felt completely at ease there. It would have been nice to have my own space and live by my own rules. I also expected to see the family more often and therefore have more opportunities to practise my French, but I barely ever saw them!

Naomi (Buenos Aires, Argentina): I think I was quite practically prepared, but maybe a bit more mental preparation would've been a good idea. When I arrived, I didn't know anyone, and found settling into a completely new continent by myself pretty difficult. I won't lie, I cried quite a lot, and really didn't want to be here to begin with. I think maybe by reaching out to a few people before coming, and keeping busy a bit more (I came two weeks before my job started, which I thought would give me more prep time but actually just made me feel a bit lost), I could have made life a bit easier for myself. And just not expecting to love it straight away. Moving across the world isn't easy – so don't expect it to be.

Maddey (Canada): I would prepare differently mentally. I expected it to be the best year of my life, for it to be really easy to make friends who I would then be besties with immediately and that I'd settle in super-easily. In reality, it was just like starting uni again, with the same difficulties of making friends and settling in, on top of cultural differences and homesickness.

How easy was it to have a social life in your new home?

Jade (San Francisco, US): I threw myself into extra-curricular activities, meeting people in my hallway and starting random conversations in the kitchen, so it felt quite easy at the start. There's definitely something to be said for approaching university with an open mindset and a willingness to make connections, even if they feel superficial at first. I really recommend getting out of your comfort zone by scheduling 'friend dates' with random people. Going for coffee, walking in the park or studying together is a good way of getting to know someone one-on-one.

Gaby (Paris, France): Unfortunately I found it very hard to make French friends, especially as I was doing an internship and wasn't studying alongside them. Thankfully, though, there was a big UK student community, so I managed to have a very good social life. Although, having a social life in Paris was very expensive – thank God for the Erasmus grant!

Naomi (Buenos Aires, Argentina): I chose a shared house of six international students, all girls, four Brits. We banded together, and from there we began to build a group based on various loose connections each person had to someone else in the city, who then introduced us to their friends, and so on and so on. But I've also made a good number of Spanish-speaking and Argentinian friends – through joining things like a boxing gym, and making an effort with colleagues in the office and at social events.

Maddey (Canada): It was quite difficult [to make friends] at first because I'm not a hugely confident person, so socialising in a new university, new city and new country was really hard. However, I joined a couple of clubs and went to some international student events and eventually got myself into a group of other exchange students who had similar personalities to myself and started doing stuff with them, not just going out to clubs but also playing board games, sports and just socialising with them, which was great.

Henry (Paris, France): It was tough [to make friends], but the best decision I made was joining a sports team. There I found that everyone had at least one thing in common – their enjoyment of rugby. Once you find like-minded individuals, the language isn't anything like the same kind of barrier.

Ellen (Lima, Peru): I got so lonely and my mental health definitely took a downward turn. I knew no one my own age; the children of my first family [in Arequipa] were indifferent about having an English girl in their house, and I was told I couldn't go out at night by myself (it got dark at 6 p.m.). However, I then moved to Lima for the second half of my placement and had the time of my life. I fell in love with the city's energy and pace of life and could finally meet up with the friends I had made. I truly appreciate having people around me now; it makes such a difference being able to spend time with people who have had the same problems and experiences you have, rather than doing everything by yourself.

Laura (Pisa, Italy): As an Erasmus student it was very easy; there were lots of events each week and most people spoke English.

What was your accommodation like?

Jade (San Francisco, US): Perhaps the biggest thing about US university is having roommates. Initially, I didn't know how to feel about it. The idea of having less personal space, navigating living preferences, etc., wasn't fun. However, I can genuinely say now that I prefer it. My two roommates are from Vietnam and Nigeria and they're wonderful. More than anything, I love our chats in the evenings. It's a great way for me to get out of my head when I'm stressed. I definitely feel like I still have personal space, especially as I spend a lot of the day alone in the city.

Naomi (Buenos Aires, Argentina): Expensive.

Paddy (Taipei, Taiwan): Accommodation was cheap, but pretty average. Just try to do your research, and if you are worried about it, try booking your flights out a week early and stay in a hotel while you look for somewhere to live. It is much easier on the ground than it is on the internet.

Maddey (Canada): My accommodation was student accommodation on campus, in a flat of four in a building mostly made up of exchange students and international students, which was nice because it meant that I got to meet lots of other people in my situation. It was also a bit annoying because I didn't meet so many local Canadians.

Henry (Paris, France): I decided to live with a French family. I lived in their spare bedroom. I have heard good and bad stories from people who did the same. Mine was a complete success story. I'm still in touch with the family now.

Ellen (Lima, Peru): Living with a host family can be such a gamble. My family in Lima were so keen to get me involved in their lives and I had my own key and we ate dinner together every night. It is definitely a cheaper option than looking at renting your own place. Also, that feeling of connecting with people whose lives are completely different to yours is what your year abroad is all about.

What did you forget to pack, which turned out to be essential?

Gaby (Paris, France): I forgot to take an overnight bag; easily solved, but I could have avoided spending €30. It's been very useful for weekend trips home and away.

Maddey (Canada): British tea – it is sold in Canada, but it's unbelievably expensive, and Canadian tea is terrible. When I got sent Yorkshire Tea in a food parcel, it was honestly one of my favourite days!

Laura (Pisa, Italy): Jaffa Cakes, wet wipes, Savlon. Insect repellent. Bedding for when it gets cold. But these are all things you can find if you look hard enough!

Were you able to travel around?

Jade (San Francisco, US): Yes! Exploring has been one of the best parts of living in the US. For fall break, some of my friends and I rented a car and road-tripped to Lake Tahoe in northern California. We stayed in a beautiful Airbnb in the middle of the forest, went hiking, paddle-boarding on the lake and generally detoxed from assignments.

Naomi (Buenos Aires, Argentina): Yes! I plan to spend two months backpacking, starting from the southernmost point of Patagonia (Ushuaia) and going all the way to Ecuador! But make sure you budget/save for this – your student loan almost certainly won't cover it.

Maddey (Canada): I did manage to travel around but sadly not as much as I would have liked, because travelling was more expensive than I expected.

Laura (Pisa, Italy): As an Erasmus student I had a lot of free time and could easily skip lectures without getting in trouble! I went to Florence, Rome, Lucca, Cinque Terre and Milan.

Did you manage to get a job while you were abroad?

Gaby (Paris, France): I interned with IMG Artists for six months. I was very lucky in my experience, I think, as they have been employing students from my university for the past 10 years or so, so there was a very smooth system (as French bureaucracy is notoriously slow) in place. They were very friendly and made me feel very welcome. They also introduced me to the world of opera; I came home feeling very cultured and with a new interest.

Paddy (Taipei, Taiwan): I have many jobs. Mostly centred around teaching English or editing English work.

Maddey (Canada): I hoped to get a job to help pay for travel and I also hoped to get some work experience, but I found out when I was there that my visa didn't allow me to work at all, except on campus, and I was unsuccessful getting any jobs there, so that was really annoying.

Laura (Pisa, Italy): I know a few people who got babysitter jobs. Parents are very keen for English-speaking babysitters and this helped keep a steady income, improve language skills and help ease loneliness.

What would be your top tips for someone else who is about to enrol?

Jade (San Francisco, US): Get ready for an intense ride! Intense academics, intense social life, intense city immersion and intense culture shock. But intense in the best way. I think speaking to current students is also crucial in understanding what student life is like.

Naomi (Buenos Aires, Argentina): I know it's clichéd, but say yes to everything. Don't let an opportunity pass; time goes soooo quickly and you only get one year abroad!

Paddy (Taipei, Taiwan): It is scary. There are going to be times when you are sitting in your room, on the other side of the world, with no mates and so many problems. And you are going to think, 'I am so lost, I don't speak the language, wtf am I doing here?' But stick with it. Because it is a massively positive experience 99 times out of 100 and will massively change your world view, which is so, so valuable.

Maddey (Canada): Bring some things from home to decorate your room with to help you settle in (e.g. duvet cover, teddy, photos, posters, bunting, etc.).

Henry (Paris, France): STICK WITH IT. The start is always tricky. You'll be homesick and you need to get everything set up: bank accounts, finding a house, meeting new people. There's a lot to do! Just persevere, because the hardest part is most often the start … JOIN CLUBS. It's a fantastic way of meeting new people!

Ellen (Lima, Peru): Find yoga classes, dance classes and language lessons wherever you are and make some friends. A place only starts to feel like home once you make it your own and you have your favourite coffee place, restaurant and running route, so try everything and establish a routine.

Laura (Pisa, Italy): Try not to compare your experience to that of someone else, especially if what you are seeing is through Instagram or other social media (no one posts about their bad days online).

Did your language skills improve?

Gaby (Paris, France): I was fully immersed in the French language from day one. Obviously, it was scary at first and I didn't understand everything, but I rapidly improved and got into the swing of things.

Naomi (Buenos Aires, Argentina): I was surprised by the number of people who just took one look at me and spoke English, and one of my jobs was also working for an English employer – so getting a second job in an all-Spanish-speaking office was a good move. I also took up an hour of cheap and relaxed Spanish classes once a week, which I would definitely recommend doing to keep yourself accountable for your progress. I've been to a couple of language mixers (social events for practising languages, called *Mundo Lingo* here) and made an effort to make Argentinian – or at least Spanish-speaking – friends, so I can try to keep improving as much as possible.

Henry (Paris, France): Yes! Particularly towards the end. I also grew to really like and appreciate the culture of my host country. I'd listen to French songs and try to watch French films ... Not only did my language improve, but I felt more 'French'.

Ellen (Lima, Peru): Absolutely. I have studied Spanish since I was five and only now would I say I am fluent. While at the time all the issues I had with host families, dealing with visa issues and general year-abroad problems felt like a massive weight, in retrospect the fact that I had to deal with everything in Spanish forced me to improve.

Laura (Pisa, Italy): Eventually! In Pisa, the only Italian I spoke was in lectures and on one (accidental) date with an Italian boy! The rest of the time I spoke English, since it's the common language for Erasmus students.

Any funny stories you can share?

Paddy (Taipei, Taiwan): Probably my favourite thing to happen was my very hard-working roommate telling me, in very broken English, that 'you have no work ethic, you have play ethic' after I came back from a night out at 7.30 a.m. to see him already up and studying.

Henry (Paris, France): My favourite one is my misuse of a particular word ... I'll set the scene: I was playing for my French university's rugby team in a semi-final of a big rugby tournament. I was normally quiet because of my poor French, but I felt like if I said just a sentence the others would understand how much this meant to me ... (the idea that even the exchange student understands the importance of the game). I started by saying, '*Je suis très excité*,' but before I could say anything else, everyone was in hysterics. I thought it meant excited, but it turns out that I had just told the team I was extremely sexually aroused.

Naomi (Buenos Aires, Argentina): In about the second week of my internship at Delicias de Alicia (a social project that teaches healthy vegetarian cooking to those in impoverished communities), my boss was asked to be on *Who Wants to Be a Millionaire*, to compete and talk about the work the organisation does, and we got to go to see it being filmed!

Laura (Pisa, Italy): I was so nervous on my first day in Pisa that I threw up into the river, in broad daylight, surrounded by horrified tourists.

Diversity at university

In order to refer to this book as a 'complete guide to university', I must first accept my own limitations as an author. My time at uni has been unique, as every experience of university is, and so there comes a point where my voice alone is not enough. This is why I felt it was important to pass the mic to people who are grossly underrepresented in higher education due to their race. I asked Renée and Ehis what their experience at university has been like.

Do you think there is a lack of diversity at university, especially at the top universities?

Renée (Cambridge and Harvard): Structurally speaking, minorities still face a number of barriers to higher education, which start long before even conceiving of a university education. From implicit biases in the school system, lower predicted grades despite overachieving, and unequipped and under-resourced schools — by the time minorities decide they want to go to university, they've already ruled themselves out.

Ehis (King's College London): There is a lack of diversity at top universities because many of them fail to create diverse and inclusive campuses, and students notice this by simply looking at pictures of the members on rugby teams or even the range of predominantly Eurocentric modules the course has to offer.

How has this impacted you personally? Were there psychological consequences?

Renée (Cambridge and Harvard): Definitely. Imposter syndrome is a real thing, especially for non-white and non-heterosexual populations. Because our identities are not normalised, and are perceived as actively different, we constantly wrestle with whether we fit in both culturally and intellectually, simply because we are different. It's crazy if you think about it, because usually it's our differences that make us positively stand out in admissions.

Ehis (King's College London): I was very prepared to withdraw my application, as I didn't want to become the spokesperson for all things black in a predominantly white space. I didn't want to walk around campus and have eyes questioning my presence there. I didn't want the consistent mispronunciation of both my first and second name. So I created this mental bubble that I shouldn't be studying and didn't deserve to even be at these institutions. Even while enrolling at King's and moving into student halls, it continued playing at the back of my mind. 'You, Ehis, are an outsider, intruding on someone else's place, and you'll get

215

caught soon.' It took a whole year to unlearn the initial mentality I came with.

Were you ever made to feel like an outsider? If so, by whom?

Renée (Cambridge and Harvard): Definitely, and not always intentionally. Sometimes the cultural norms just weren't for me. I'm not a heavy drinker. I don't like croquet – ha-ha. I don't like rock music, or anything electric or pop. I love cooking African food. I speak slang here and there. It was hard sometimes because in a lot of situations I found myself to be the only black woman from a particular background in a room of predominantly white people. It was tough because even when I tried to adopt mannerisms and certain cultural elements, it didn't work organically for me. But soon I embraced my differences, and that's when I felt most comfortable. That's when the people around me also enjoyed my company the most, funnily enough.

Ehis (King's College London): The greatest misconception people have when black students or students of other ethnic backgrounds say they feel like outsiders is that students of the white majority consciously or purposefully did something to exclude these students. This is often not the case, as a lot happens subconsciously. I believe it is nearly impossible to exist as a black boy in these spaces and to not feel like an outsider. Additionally – this one is a little trickier to explain – but sometimes you're even made to feel like an outsider when the majority makes an attempt to include you. Let's say the seminar somehow manages to take a turn to discuss post-war colonialism in West Africa, or there is a debate about who the better rapper is between J. Cole and Kendrick Lamar during lunchtime, and everyone suddenly turns to you to be the spokesman during the conversation, as if your opinion is the final verdict. That moment right there leads to this queasy feeling where you would rather the ground just open up and take you with it, as suddenly you're now the diplomat for all things black, be it history, politics or culture (even if you don't know anything about the issue at hand).

Were there ways of finding people you could relate to when you felt most alone?

Renée (Cambridge and Harvard): Affinity groups were SO important to my university experience. I joined women's groups. I became president of the African and Caribbean Society. ACS, in particular, was my lifeline. I made some of the best and most deep friendships there, because they truly resonated with my experience.

Did the education system and curriculum fail to represent you or the areas of study you were interested in?

Renée (Cambridge and Harvard): In primary school and secondary school I never learned much about Africa or India, bar one module. In university it was better, and it's getting better, too. I studied history and now they are really implementing the Global South into the curriculum – crucially not as a niche but a real main topic.

Ehis (King's College London): Between 2016 and 2017, there were 25 black women and 90 black men among the 19,000 professors in the United Kingdom – I'm sure the disparity in numbers speaks for itself. But this debate then evolves to go around in a full circle. For there to be more professors from a black or ethnic background, we need more students going into further education. However, they won't do so if the curriculum doesn't spark their interest or they don't believe higher education is for them. But overall, yes. The curriculum is incredibly Eurocentric and sometimes does indeed fail to represent myself and the areas of study I'm interested in.

How can institutions ensure that they are facilitating diversity?

Ehis (King's College London): Personally, I think there are so many ways universities can facilitate diversity, but the question is whether these institutions care to do so. I'm writing this in October, which is meant to be Black History Month, and if I'm being completely honest a lot of universities literally operate below the bare minimum. You might get a cheeky poster of Rosa Parks on a noticeboard, alongside a picture of Martin Luther King Jr during the March on Washington for Jobs and Freedom, where he delivered the 'I have a Dream ...' speech in 1963, and if you're really lucky you might get a quote from Malcom X, as long as the Students' Union didn't find it too radical. And that right there is the problem. There is so much more that can be done, from employing student ambassadors who focus on the awareness around diversity to actually investing time and money (alongside creative and modern ideas) into PR and working with societies whose fundamental reason for existence is to support minorities and fund their plans and events. There's so much that can be done, and I don't want to write a complete action plan, because my main issue is given in my first sentence – do these institutions care?

How can people who would be considered part of a majority be better allies to those who are not?

Renée (Cambridge and Harvard): The first port of call is to try to hear people out and understand how vastly different their experiences are. Never assume or generalise. Ensure that you are empathetic and take the time to really get to know the basic issues facing a community, and then layer on top of that. Advocate on their terms. Do not jump the gun or centre yourself in conversations or situations that you see are serving injustice. Try to speak up for people, but then hand the microphone to the people who are actually in need of that platform.

Ehis (King's College London):
1. **Understand that racism is everywhere.** I know that sounds a bit intimidating, but in the same way we look at sociological factors, such as gender, sex and social class, or the presence of economic and political influence on areas of life, always understand that racism is everywhere, and it happens every day.
2. **Speak up!** Sometimes the problem isn't that some members of the majority are those primarily being racist, but the issue lies in choosing to be silent. I will never forget the day a girl in my seminar – who, prior to this, I had never really spoken to outside of the occasional 'Did you do the reading?' – called out a

seminar tutor for somehow being able to pronounce every single person's name perfectly but yet came with a different variant of my name every single seminar and made no effort to learn it. When you see something wrong, don't justify it – question it. A good book on this is *Race Talk and the Conspiracy of Silence: Understanding and Facilitating Difficult Dialogues on Race* by Derald Wing Sue.

3. **Educate yourself.** Understand your position as a member of a majority and why there is an existence of a minority. Come to terms with the fact that there is such a thing as white superiority and understand white racial identity. Learn how racism has evolved over time and has become much more subverted. Ask questions. The corny stereotypes are not the narratives you should be running with. Don't assume; literally ask what you need to know and share that information with other members of the majority.

4. **Read, research and listen.** This could have been part of my third point, but I wanted to highlight that it was only through reading that I understood the concept of racial intersectionality. In simple terms: yes, it's kinda hard being a black heterosexual man (however, the patriarchy still benefits me). It's harder being a black Muslim woman. So understand that there are connections between racism, homophobia, sexism, economic issues and other forms of injustice.

Are there any books or studies you could recommend for people wanting to find out more?

Renée (Cambridge and Harvard):

1. *Why I'm No Longer Talking to White People About Race* by Reni Eddo-Lodge (Bloomsbury, 2018)
2. *Taking Up Space: The Black Girl's Manifesto for Change* by Chelsea Kwakye and Ore Ogunbiyi (Merky Books, 2019)

Ehis (King's College London):

1. *The New Jim Crow: Mass Incarceration in the Age of Colourblindness* by Michelle Alexander (Penguin, 2019)
2. *The Diversity Delusion* by Heather Mac Donald (Macmillan, 2018)
3. *Can We Talk About Race? And Other Conversations in an Era of School Resegregation* by Dr Beverly Daniel Tatum (Beacon Press, 2008)
4. *White Fragility: Why It's So Hard for White People to Talk About Racism* by Robin Diangelo (Penguin, 2019)
5. *Witnessing Whiteness: The Need to Talk About Race and How to Do It* by Shelly Tochluk (R&L Education, 2010)
6. *Race Talk and the Conspiracy of Silence: Understanding and Facilitating Difficult Dialogues on Race* by Derald Wing Sue (Wiley, 2016)

7. *Understanding White Privilege: Creating Pathways to Authentic Relationships Across Race* by Frances E. Kendall (Routledge, 2013)

CHAPTER 7

WELLBEING

It's important to look after yourself at university, and I don't just mean making sure your clothes are clean and that your diet consists of something that isn't a Pot Noodle. You've got to be kind to your mental health, too. Remember that you're never, ever alone, and even though sometimes it can be tough, it's okay to admit that you're struggling. I hope this section can help you in times of need.

Let's talk about mental health

Everyone has mental health. Regardless of its past, present or future condition, everyone has mental health, just as we all have physical health.

Except that our mental health is invisible. It exists in a place where the naked eye cannot see it, and this makes it far more difficult to comprehend and translate. It's a braille only you can read, but there's also no one to teach you how to do this.

Just like skin, everyone has mental health. Yet when someone's skin is cut or bruised or bleeding, we sympathise – even empathise – with this pain. We want to help because we understand that they are suffering.

With the skin that clothes our *own* bodies, physical scratches and discomforts are validated, because they are seen. By ourselves and by others. This suffering is universally understood *as* suffering.

But when the metaphorical skin of mental health is scratched or tarnished, we fail to register and recognise it in ourselves and in others. It's tricky to empathise or understand because the wound doesn't bleed; the point of impact doesn't turn purple and blue and green. It's invisible, and impacts us so individually that it's hard to even understand.

But this mental-health 'skin' can certainly be scarred. It can suddenly flare up when triggered by something it is intolerant to. It can also be clear and untainted right now, but that doesn't mean it will stay that way forever. Equally, cuts and bruises will clear up with the right care, though they may leave a vulnerability behind. Mental-health struggles operate in the same way as physical pain – they're just internal rather than external.

One in four people in the UK will experience a mental health problem each year. Four in every four people in the UK *have* mental health.

It's not a one-time thing and it's not a sometimes-I-have-mental-health-and-other-times-I'm-fine kind of deal. You always have mental health, and you always need to look after it. But it's not your fault if that task becomes impossible.

Check in with your friends. Check in with your family. Check in with yourself. The only way we can care for this skin is by, firstly, recognising that it's there and, secondly, taking measures to look after it.

Everyone has mental health.

Mental health: Some things you can do to look after yourself

1. Think of an easy theme like animals, cities, countries or names and then go through the alphabet and come up with something within the category that starts with each letter. It sounds simple, but that's the charm of it. This activity will take your brain to a completely different place and give you a short-term focus, which is incredibly straightforward. It's great for just calming yourself down if necessary.

2. Place your left hand flat in front of you and spread your fingers. Now trace it using your right index finger. As you move up each finger on the left hand, inhale, and as you move back down the finger, exhale. Give yourself time to just breathe and really focus on it. This is especially good in an exam or public setting, as it's so discreet.

3. Use the Headspace app to focus on mindfulness and meditation. A silky-smooth voice guides you through the session – which can be as long or as short as you want – and there's also meditations for beginners, which are only 2–3 minutes long.

4. If you're not yet ready to talk to someone, give this a try: get a scrap piece of paper or a 'notes' page on your laptop/phone and write down everything that is overwhelming you. Get it all out, vent, rage ... and then destroy it. Delete the document, rip up the paper, burn it if that's what gives you closure. Physically annihilate the issues that are overwhelming you, and perhaps it'll help to give you some closure. Plus, writing everything down might help you get your head around things, in the same way that talking to someone would.

Imposter syndrome at university

There is one thing I haven't addressed so far in this book that has impacted me just as much, if not more, than most of the other topics I've discussed in these pages. It's been as big a part of my uni experience as the sports I've played, the places I've lived and the people I've met ... but it's not quite as pretty. In fact, it's not something I've ever talked about, whether that's within the confines of this book, on my YouTube channel or just in the real, everyday world. But this is a university survival guide, and this is the struggle I have had to survive. So I'd like to finally introduce you to: my imposter syndrome.

I left secondary school and sixth form feeling pretty confident in my academic ability. Sure, I had a kaleidoscope of butterflies on A Level results day, and my fair share of 'see me after class' notes scrawled on some hastily written – and entirely useless – essays, but I was, generally speaking, pretty self-assured that I *could* do it, and that the sky was the limit in terms of academic achievement. I never walked into a class feeling insecure, or like not knowing an answer would render me the stupidest person in the room, nor did I think that anyone had this attitude towards anybody else. I didn't tremble at the thought of putting my hand up to ask to have something clarified, or struggle to force myself to attend lessons crippled by the prospect of being picked on and not knowing an answer. I wasn't afraid to be wrong, or to try, or to be part of a learning process.

Now I'm at university, I don't recognise that person.

In the three years of my degree, I have actively distanced myself from people who study the same subject as me. I sit on my own, at the very, very back, in lectures. I rarely have the confidence to speak in tutorials or seminars. And I would never, *ever* discuss my opinions on a book or lecture with my peers. I have isolated myself from the people who share the most common interests to me, and I have missed out on so much friendship, learning and growth because of it.

The reason for this is that, from the very first English lecture I walked into, I felt like I wasn't good enough. My brain has convinced me that I am the least intelligent person in the room; the bottom of the food chain; a meerkat in a room of hyenas, cackling at my expense. Whenever I think I know the answer to a question, something inside me holds me back, like a burly bouncer outside a nightclub at full capacity, and makes me second-guess myself. I genuinely believe that the other people in the room have more of a right to be there and share their opinions.

I feel like an imposter. Like I don't belong there. Like I didn't earn my place as everyone else did. Like I won some sort of competition. And that everyone else knows it.

I feel like I stick out like a lamb shank at a vegan festival.

This all happened to me almost subconsciously. I can't even pinpoint a specific moment when I chose to isolate myself on a course of 250 other people who were arguably very similar to me. Even as I write this, in my third year, I know that in an hour's time, when I go to my lecture today, I will actively try to sit on my own so that no one asks me what I thought of the book we're studying or reads my lecture notes, because I'll be intrinsically ashamed of them. In the tutorial following this, I will probably not say a word, making it look like I didn't prepare at all, despite slaving over research for three hours in the library this morning.

Only in the first month of this academic year did I even begin to realise that the way I felt had a name – imposter syndrome – which I could completely identify with. For one of my modules, we are being taken on a field trip to the oldest working Georgian theatre in the UK, which is in Richmond, Yorkshire, for a series of lectures on eighteenth-century drama in the place it was actually performed. This should be an exciting prospect, to go on a school trip as a university student, and yet I am absolutely dreading it because of the bus journey where I will embarrassingly sit alone, the lunch break where I'll inevitably be a complete loner, and the sad fact that I probably won't speak to a single soul all day. This feeling has been so normal to me for such a long time that I don't even register it as a problem any more; it's just a general academic insecurity and social fear, which are permanent residents within my brain.

Fundamentally – escaping my godawful mind for a moment – none of these things are true. Objectively speaking, I did get the grades to go to university, and I have managed to pass every year so far (even getting a first in my second year), just like every one of my peers. The reality is that not a single one of the people on my course will think that I don't deserve to be here, and many of them will probably secretly feel the same way I do. These people are too busy thinking about their own last-minute essays and the 9 a.m. tutorials they haven't prepared for to even pay attention to me. In a way, it was kind of ridiculous to even assume that anyone was giving a second thought to what I was doing – let alone giving a toss about my academic prowess. But, unfortunately, brains don't work in such a rational way as this.

You know that field trip I spoke about before? I hope you do, as it was literally two paragraphs ago. (I know we've spoken about how to skim-read and fly through your reading piles, but that doesn't apply to this book, okay?) Well, since writing that paragraph, I went on it. What actually transpired was that someone came and sat next to me on the bus straight away. We had a really great chat about the course, our dissertations, how we were finding the workload and – best of all – how truly and utterly clueless we *both* were. That lunch break I was dreading? I got chatting to some other people on the trip, who, it turns out, I share many mutual friends with, and we all went out for a really tasty lunch together. I wasn't stuck in miserable silence all day; I came home elated that I'd made proper course friends for the first time in three years. This was the confidence boost I needed to live my best life at university within the social space of my degree, and to stop feeling so petrified of looking dumb, or disorganised, or like I don't deserve to be there.

I've had this bizarre inferiority complex for years, which I'd never experienced academically before, and it's time to get out of that rut. Going from being pretty near the top of my class at school to being in a room full of people with exactly the same ability as me was intimidating and scary, and it's tough to suddenly feel vulnerable and insecure when academia has always been *your thing*. But I'm working on it, and if you're feeling the same way, take this as your pivotal moment when you turn things around.

Firstly, it's okay to admit that you're struggling. I remember feeling like a complete fool in my 'Germanic Myth and Legend' module, which I took because it sounded fascinating, because everyone else already seemed to know every single intimate detail of mythology before we even started studying it, to the point where I wondered whether divine intervention was actually assisting them. Everyone always seemed to have read twelve more books than I had, and to have nine days in their week to study compared to my measly seven. If I'd been to Tenerife, they'd been to Elevenerife. In situations like these, the answer is to just talk to your tutor. They will understand and be able to help, and will probably point you towards the books and information you need to plug those gaps in your knowledge.

Secondly, don't expect to be the finished product already. I'm convinced university is just three or four years of pretending you know what you're doing, and most of the people who are flexing their encyclopaedic knowledge probably read what they're telling you five minutes before, or know nothing about something you've researched thoroughly. We're here to learn, improve and be enlightened, and anyone who believes they're already an expert will probably be so closed-minded that they won't ever achieve the top grades.

Thirdly, remember that your reading, research and areas of specialisation will be totally different to everyone else's. The nature of undergraduate-level research is that you are constantly falling down rabbit holes and connecting the dots between the unique constellations of things you know. Believe me, you know things your peers don't have a clue about, just as they know about certain things in fantastic depth that you aren't aware of. It's so impossible to compare yourself to others that there's really no point in trying.

Finally, and I know this is so clichéd that it belongs in Comic Sans on a poster of a waterfall or a sunset, but *believe in yourself*. You've earned your right to be at that institution, whether you got the grades, got there through clearing, transferred from another uni or are starting your undergraduate degree in your thirties. You're there because you deserve to be, regardless of what anyone says or what you convince yourself anyone else is thinking. We're all on our own individual journeys, living this experience, and you are valid and worthy and incredible. So start believing it.

Where to find help
if you need it

Nightline: Nightline is a confidential, anonymous, non-judgmental, non-directive and non-advisory support service run by students for students. They will listen to you talk no matter what time of night, over instant messages, emails or calls, and all volunteers are students, so they can empathise with what you're experiencing. www.nightline.ac.uk/want-to-talk.

Samaritans: A registered charity aimed at providing emotional support for anyone struggling to cope or at risk of suicide in the UK and Ireland. They offer a telephone helpline for immediate support. Call 116 123 or visit www.samaritans. org.

CALM: Campaign Against Living Miserably is a mental health charity that offers help, advice and information to anyone who is struggling or in crisis. They have a free, confidential and anonymous helpline as well as a webchat, which is open daily from 5 p.m. till midnight. Call 0800 585858 or visit www.thecalmzone.net.

Headspace: A fantastic mindfulness app with loads of different guided meditations, specialising on a variety of wonderful topics. There's also a beginners' course, which is a good gateway to practising meditation – don't knock it till you try it! Search for 'Headspace' on your app store.

NHS: The National Health Service is one of the best things about this country, and a resource which should be utilised when looking after your mental health. Try to book an appointment if necessary, but if the waiting times are long, check out their website for advice, explanations and information on mental health. Visit www.nhs.uk.

Blue Thoughts: A website set up by the singer Lauv, where people around the globe can share their thoughts anonymously, both for the relief and catharsis of sharing and to remind others that they are not alone. You can search keywords or search by country to see other people's thoughts on things like loneliness, homesickness and heartbreak, as well as share your own ideas. Visit www.mybluethoughts. world.

Kooth: A confidential mental health advice website, specifically aimed at children and young people. You can chat to counsellors and read articles written by fellow young people about mental health, which may make the way you're feeling a bit more manageable. Visit www.kooth.com.

The university: Check out your university's website to find out what internal support systems they offer. I'll be real with you, often the waiting times are long, but getting on to the waiting list is still a step in the right direction. Look into the other steps here for more short-term solutions, but still contact the university as well.

CONCLUSION

Thank you for joining me in The Uni-Verse – a year-long passion project I compiled and wrote over the course of the final year of my own university experience.

As I draw my own undergraduate degree to a close, it feels quite apt to write the survival guide I would've wanted to read three years ago. I hope this book helps reassure you that university is the best option for you, helps clear up some of the misconceptions or questions you had, and excites you to get started.

I'll leave you with a letter I've written to my pre-fresher self, who desperately needed it.

Dear 2017 Jack,
It's the day before move-in day. You're shaking with anxiety, your teeth are chattering and your legs are trembling (much to the annoyance of everyone around you). With every moment, you're getting one step closer to confessing that you don't want to go to

university after all, because you're, quite frankly, shitting it. It's been your dream to go to uni from the moment you knew what it was, but suddenly, now the moment is upon you, a tidal wave of dread has you submerged. You're terrified. Terrified of not fitting in. Terrified of not being good enough. Terrified of not being able to keep yourself alive.

Well, you did it. You made it to university, even though every fibre of your being was convincing you that it wouldn't live up to expectation, because you didn't *deserve* to be there. You made it to the end of your first year, somehow consuming your body weight in vodka every term without being hospitalised. You then made it through second year, and truly fell in love with your degree. By your third year you'd started to realise that, actually, maybe this was the best decision of your whole entire life.

Looking back from the vantage point of being within touching distance of graduation, I'm so glad that everything worked out the way it did.

You're going to meet the most incredible, inspiring and interesting people from all over the country – and all over the world – who will be friends for life. You will experience the most wonderfully chaotic years together and rely on one another when you need it most. That's a different kind of bond.

You're going to have opportunities you'll never forget, and you're going to love every second of it.

There will be snow days where you sled down a hill on an old ladder you found in the woods. There will be days you write off because you're too hungover to move or wear anything other than a dressing gown. There will be questionable decisions and questionable fancy dress. There will be parties, spontaneous bar nights (which always turn into the best ones) and deep chats with your housemates before one of you realises it's 3 a.m. and time to get some sleep. Suddenly that 9 a.m. lecture is looking less appealing ...

It's going to be hard. It's going to be overwhelming and intense. It's going to push you to new limits you didn't even know you could reach. But it's also going to make you the best version of yourself. It's going to turn you into someone you might even be proud of.

Power on ... you've got this. And it'll all be worth it.

2020 Jack

SOME RECOMMENDATIONS

Books

- Chelsea Kwakye and Ore Ogunbiyi, *Taking Up Space: The Black Girl's Manifesto for Change* (Merky Books, 2019)
- Charlotte Pike, *The Hungry Student Cookbook* (Quercus, 2013)
- Bethie Hungerford, *The Hungerpots Cookbook* (HarperCollins, 2020)
- Malcolm Gladwell, *Outliers: The Story of Success* (Penguin, 2009)
- Zadie Smith, *On Beauty* (Penguin, 2006)
- Adam Kay, *This Is Going to Hurt: Secret Diaries of a Junior Doctor* (Picador, 2018)

Podcasts

- The Wooden Spoon (my podcast redefining success and failure)
- Radio 1's Life Hacks (honest chats about big issues impacting young people)
- TED Talks Daily (insightful talks by the world's most interesting people)
- No Such Thing As a Fish (hilarious podcast packed with bizarre facts)
- Myths and Legends (captivating tales from global mythology and folklore)
- Song Exploder (complete escapism – your favourite artists deconstruct their music)
- George Ezra & Friends (a fascinating insight into the music industry)
- My Dad Wrote a Porno (as outrageous as it sounds)
- Today in Focus (go behind the headlines of the *Guardian*)
- Happy Place (Fearne Cotton's wonderful podcast about mental health)
- Desert Island Discs (eight tracks, a book and a luxury you'd take to a desert island)
- The Guilty Feminist (comedy podcast with thought-provoking discussions)

YouTube channels

- Eve Cornwell (studied at Bristol University, now a trainee lawyer)
- Ruby Granger (studying at Exeter University)
- UnJaded Jade (studying in San Francisco)
- Ehis Ilozobhie (studying at King's College London)
- Derin Adetosoye (studying at the London College of Fashion)
- Eve Bennett (studying at Oxford University)
- Vee Kativhu (studying at Oxford University)
- Ibz Mo (studied at Cambridge University, now studying law)
- Luke Birch (studying at Lincoln University)
- Lydia Violeta (studying at Leeds University)
- Molly Thompson (studied at Leeds University)
- Maninder Sachdeva (studying at Oxford University)
- Viola Helen (studying at Oxford University)
- Joe Binder (studied at Cambridge University)
- Rosie Crawford (studied at Oxford University)
- Laur Medley (studying at sixth form)
- Luke Catleugh (studied at University of the Arts London)

ACKNOWLEDGEMENTS

Firstly – because they'd kill me if they weren't first – Mum and Dad. Thank you for giving up your time to ferry me around the country for every university open day, and for empathising with all the silly worries I had. Thank you for always being at the other end of the phone to give advice I didn't want to hear but desperately needed. Thank you for teaching me that compassion, kindness and hard work will get you where you want to be. Most importantly, thank you for sending me pictures of the dog whenever I felt homesick.

To my brother, Adam, for conveniently deciding to go to university just as I was writing a guide for freshers – you really did me a solid with that one. Half the content in this book comes from the questions you asked me.

Thank you to the rest of my family, too, for always checking in on me and motivating me to keep going. Especially, thank you to my wonderful grandparents who have always and will always be my biggest inspiration. Also, I'm sorry that the concept of your grandson filming his life and putting it on the internet is tricky to explain to your friends … they definitely think I make adult movies. At least you can say 'author' from now on.

Thank you to my university family, who made this experience the most special and treasured time of my life. Ella, Will and Emma, where do I even begin? You've been my rocks since day one and it's been a privilege to share a home with you for three years – one by accident, two by choice. It's tricky to put into words just how important you are to me, but I hope you know I couldn't have done this without you.

To my incredible girlfriend, Sammy – I'm not sure what I did to deserve you, but I'll be forever grateful that you extended the enormous amount of charity work you do to dating me. You're the most thoughtful, caring and beautiful person … Now it's in print you'd better believe it.

Josie, Lucy, Emma D, Charlie, Phil and Badger the cat, I'm so lucky to have been arbitrarily allocated to House 12, South Bailey, and to have spent my first year with you. From sliding down the stairs on our mattresses to (unknowingly) adorning the house with asbestos-ridden Christmas decorations, we made that temporary house feel like home. Even if I did lock myself out of it every other day.

Adam, Lydia, Rachel, Giles, Martha, Jenny, Lucy B, Zahra, Maddy, Rishi, Hatty, Mabrur, Georgia – you mean the world to me. Thank you for making every day at university so fantastic. Holly, Liam, Calum, Ed, Lauren, Joe – you'll be friends for life.

Paddy – you inspired the whole section on studying abroad thanks to your experience of turning up for university in

Taiwan, only to find that the only English course available was exclusively about the history of goats. Gaby and Alice, my final year hasn't been the same without you here. Thanks for being such a huge part of my university experience, and thanks in advance for the fact that I'll be using your new student house as a hotel every time I miss student life.

Naomi, Henry, Laura, Maddey and Ellen, thank you for your contributions to the studying abroad section and for allowing me to share your stories – I know your insights will help and reassure so many people. Renée and Ehis, your words in this book are powerful and important – thank you for opening your hearts to let me in. Ibz Mo, your advice and guidance have been invaluable. Derin, I'm so glad we're experiencing this crazy journey together.

Thank you to the amazing team at HarperCollins that I've had the privilege of working with. Omara, Lydia and Sarah, thank you for your kindness and patience. You've let me be unashamedly *me* on every single page of this book and have been so understanding of every little tweak I wanted to make. I should also add an apology: I'm sorry you had to read every shit joke that didn't make it into the book … as well as those that did. I'm not sure how many of your authors you've had to advise against using the term 'academic boner', but I'm proud to be one of them.

To the design team at HarperCollins – you made my vision for the cover come to life, and I'm so deeply in love with it. To Hattie and Lucy in publicity, and all those involved in the production and sale of my book, thank you for your hard work. You're the best in the biz and every day I consider it an honour to be working with you.

Thank you to those at talent agency Sixteenth, without whom I couldn't exist. You changed my life, and I will never, ever be able to express my gratitude enough. Nish, Max, Danny, Lauren and Mama Rachel – thank you for going above and beyond, every hour of every day.

Jade, Ruby, Eve … three of the most kind-hearted individuals I've ever had the good luck to meet. Not many people get to call their idol a close friend, but I've got three of them. Thank you for your support and empathy every step of the way, even through those 'wooden spoon' moments.

Finally, to my YouTube audience, who enabled me to craft a life I love. You have no idea how important each and every one of you are, or how many times a kind message you sent on a whim has turned my day around. None of this would exist without you. In fact, my name was first brought up to my publishers because someone who watched my videos recommended me to HarperCollins. You've made my dreams come true, and I can never, ever repay you for that. Thank you so much for the love you give to me.